AL-GHAZĀLĪ

LETTER TO A DISCIPLE

Ayyuhā 'l-Walad · bilingual English-Arabic edition translated with an Introduction & Notes by TOBIAS MAYER

Notes by TOBIAS MAYER

أيها الولد

THE ISLAMIC TEXTS SOCIETY

This edition published 2005 by
THE ISLAMIC TEXTS SOCIETY
22A Brooklands Avenue, Cambridge, CB2 2DQ, UK

ISBN–13: 978 0946621 62 0 cloth
ISBN–13: 978 0946621 63 7 paper

ISBN–10: 0946621 62 4 cloth
ISBN–10: 0946621 63 2 paper

British Library Cataloguing-in-Publication Data.
A catalogue record for this book is
available from the British Library.

Set with ArabTEX and BaKoMaTEX
in Bembo and Naskh types.
The publishers wish to thank
Prof. Klaus Lagally (Stuttgart) for his generous help.

Contents

Abbreviations	vi
Introduction	vii
I. Intellectual context	vii
II. Biographical context	xi
III. Content of *Ayyuhā 'l-walad*	xxii
IV. Arabic text of the epistle	xxxv
Notes to Introduction	xxxvii
Translation and Arabic Text	2
Notes to Translation	63
Appendix: Persons Cited in the Text	65
Bibliography	71
Index	75

Abbreviations

EI	: *Encyclopædia of Islam* (First edition)
EI²	: *Encyclopædia of Islam* (Second edition)
GAL	: Brockelmann, *Geschichte der arabischen Litteratur* 2nd ed.
GALS	: Brockelmann, *Geschichte der arabischen Litteratur* (*Supplement*)

Introduction

I. INTELLECTUAL CONTEXT

ABŪ ḤĀMID Muḥammad ibn Muḥammad al-Ghazālī is widely seen in Islam as the 'renewer' (*mujaddid*) of the 6th century AH, in line with the well-known prophetic tradition that such a figure would arise every hundred years.[A] Aside from his important contributions as a Shāfiᶜite jurist,[1] Ashᶜarite theologian,[2] and defender of Sunnī orthodoxy against Avicennism[3] and Ismāᶜīlism,[4] he is overwhelmingly linked with the medieval popularisation of the 'sober' or Junaydī kind of Sufism. The main work with which this aspect of his contribution is associated is his four volume *Revival of the Religious Sciences* (*Iḥyā' ᶜulūm al-dīn*) from which *Ayyuhā 'l-walad* quotes and of which it is a kind of epitome.

Ghazālī is the undisputed figurehead of the revived Sunnism of the Seljuq period which reversed the political dominance of various forms of Shīᶜism in the 4th/10th century. Seljuq intellectual culture emerges from a forbidding complex of pressures and influences—a complexity reflected in Ghazālī. One way in which these contemporary forces might be summarised is in terms of the challenge of 'wisdom' (*ḥikma*), variously defined, to exoteric Islam. This challenge was primarily felt on three sides.

[A] *Inna 'Llāha yabᶜathu li-hādhihi 'l-ummati ᶜalā ra'si kulli mi'ati sanatin man yujaddidu lahā dīnahu.* Abū Dāūd, *Malāḥim*, I, 424.

To begin with, Graeco-Arabic philosophy had lately been given a fulsome and incomparably authoritative expression in Islam by the great Persian thinker Avicenna or Abū ʿAlī al-Ḥusayn ibn ʿAbd Allāh Ibn Sīnā (d. 428/1037). The 6th/12th century has been referred to as a period of Avicennan epidemic, at least in eastern Islam.[5] There is indeed ample evidence for the powerful impact of Avicennism in texts from this period.[6] Ibn Sīnā had been at pains to develop Peripatetic thought in step with Islamic concerns, for example elaborating a theory of prophecy in his psychology,[7] explaining the data of Islamic eschatology within a philosophical framework,[8] and carefully keeping the language of inception (*ḥudūth*) in his cosmogony of pre-eternal instauration.[9] It was partly because of 'Islamic' refinements like these that Graeco-Arabic philosophy through Ibn Sīnā gained wide enough influence to disturb the religious establishment.

The second assault on exoteric Islam by advocates of 'wisdom' saw it take political form, a militant movement which laid claim to its own religious sanction and credentials lateral to those of Sunnism. This was Ismāʿīlī Shīʿism in which a rich philosophical system of partly Neoplatonic provenance (elaborated by thinkers like Abū Yaʿqūb al-Sijistānī[10] and Ḥamīd al-Dīn al-Kirmānī)[11] was combined with the claim of the charismatic authority of the Prophet's lineage. In Ghazālī's lifetime the sect was transformed in the Seljuq domains both doctrinally and practically into a new and fearsome movement—the Nizārī Ismāʿīlism of al-Ḥasan ibn al-Ṣabbāḥ (d. 518/1124) which would prove to be a persistent stumbling block to the Seljuqs.[12] Holding extensive territories within the Seljuq empire (e.g. Daylam, Māzandarān and Qūhistān), the Nizārīs also espoused a dramatic policy of assassination to which more than one of Ghazālī's great patrons allegedly fell victim.

The mystical dimension known as Sufism constituted the third and arguably profoundest challenge by 'wisdom' to Sunnī exoterism. Sufism's origins were disputed by earlier orientalist scholars, but their sympathy for the thesis of a primarily non-

Islamic (notably Neoplatonic or Christian) pedigree has been swept aside in favour of the contrary view that it is primarily Islamic—the prevalent claim of Sufism's exponents themselves.[A] That said, the ambiguity of the relationship of this eminently home grown form of *ḥikma* with the religion's juridical and dogmatic aspects is historically quite clear—from the various trials of mystics under the ʿAbbāsid caliphs between the 870s and the 930s right through to modern denunciations by Salafī and Wahhābī reformers. Even under Seljuq hegemony, Sufi thinkers could fall foul of the religious authorities, as shown by the trial and execution of ʿAyn al-Quḍāt al-Hamadhānī (exe. 525/1131) twenty years after Ghazālī's death.

While Sufism claimed to prolong the intense spirituality of the Prophetic and 'apostolic' era of Islam, more than one trend threatened to render its mission marginal by the 4th/10th century. On the one hand, Islam as a whole underwent an exceptionally rapid phase of scholastic elaboration in which a powerful armoury of religious sciences appeared such as Ḥadīth, jurisprudence and Kalām theology. Yet this process through which the religion became radically formalized and systematized, brilliant though it was, threatened to neglect the vital sphere of the inner life, the individual soul's deeper relationship with God. On the other hand, some mystics themselves began dramatically to emphasize the asymmetry of their interior path with exoteric religious norms, figures like Abū Yazīd al-Basṭāmī, Abū 'l-Ḥusayn al-Nūrī, Sumnūn ibn Ḥamza, Manṣūr al-Ḥallāj and the architects of the *Malāmatī* 'way of blame', Ḥamdūn al-Qaṣṣār and Abū Ḥafs ʿAmr al-Ḥaddādī.[13] Through such mystics as these a worrying tension between Sufi spirituality and official religion emerged, apparent not only in the mystics' doctrines (e.g. divine love, *theôsis*),

[A]The value of Louis Massignon's *Essai* should not be under-estimated in shifting the consensus on Sufism's origins. In this work—originally his Ph.D. thesis—Massignon comprehensively demonstrates the Qur'ānic and Islamic basis of the terms and concepts of Islamic mysticism. See L. Massignon, *Essay on the Origins of the Technical Language of Islamic Mysticism.*

but their chosen media (e.g. poetry, music, the 'theopathic utterance' or *shaṭḥ*), and their rich variety of paraliturgical practices. As mentioned, a period of overt conflict began under the ʿAbbāsid caliphs from the 870s which was mainly orchestrated by the Ḥanbalī jurist, Ghulām al-Khalīl. The most famous victim of these persecutions was undoubtedly Ḥallāj, with his two major trials in 301/913 and 309/922, resulting in his execution.[14]

Already during the Ḥallājian drama a countervailing trend had strong support in the school of thought linked with Abū 'l-Qāsim al-Junayd al-Qawārīrī (d. 298/910)—a major mystical theorist and one of a number of contemporary Sufis who joined in denouncing Ḥallāj. A central issue here was the Ḥallājian claim of *theôsis*, encapsulated in the famous *shaṭḥ 'anā 'l-Ḥaqq'*, 'I am the Truth'. Junayd betrays an obsession with the whole question in his epistles and stresses the ultimate subjectivity of the experience, which he claimed involves the mystic's 'passing away' in the Godhead (*fanā'*) in his imagination only (*ʿala 'l-tawahhum*).[15] The distinction of creature from Creator was for him non-negotiable, insofar as it was ethically and religiously foundational.

Junayd's 'sober' (*ṣaḥwī*) as distinct from 'intoxicated' (*sukrī*) mysticism heralds a reaction to the period of tension, a reaction expressed in a wave of Sufi manuals and compilations which emphasised the strict religious probity of the *via mystica* in the course of fixing its teachings and recording its lore. Composed within a relatively brief period from the mid-4th/10th century through to the mid-5th/11th century, these works,[16] which are now regarded as the classics of Islamic mystical literature, were at least partly motivated by the need to defend Sufism through establishing the complementarity of exoteric and esoteric truth. Ghazālī's momentous contribution, in the wake of these texts from this slightly earlier period, is strongly at one with their integrative agenda. Yet it is not enough to view him as simply an apologist and mediator. Ghazālī's project goes further and is, understood properly, no longer defensive. For the Ghazālian point of view insists not just on the compatibility of spheres, but that Sufism is absolutely indispensable for an authentic Islam and that in consequence the whole of the religion must be informed by the mystical impulse.

II. BIOGRAPHICAL CONTEXT

It will become clear that Ghazālī's life acutely dramatized the indispensability of Sufism for a genuine Islam and it is the personal events pertaining to this epoch-making discovery by him which will form the focus of this section. Ghazālī emerged from the Khorāsānian town of Ṭūs, held as a fief by the statesman whose shadow is cast over the whole period, Abū ʿAlī Ḥasan al-Ṭūsī, known as 'Niẓām al-Mulk' (d. 485/1092). As vizier to three of the greatest Seljuq sultans over a period of three decades, Niẓām al-Mulk is credited with orchestrating a revival of Sunnī learning through founding the system of colleges known after him as *al-madāris al-niẓāmiyya*, the Niẓāmiyya colleges. Al-Subkī lists an ultimate total of nine of these institutions which were founded in the towns of the Seljuq empire, but Ghazālī's life is especially linked with their 'mother' college on the east bank of the river Tigris in Baghdad itself.

Like other thinkers of the time, Ghazālī boasts of intellectual precocity. The interplay of exoteric and esoteric science is already clear in his early education in Ṭūs, for besides laying the groundwork for his forthcoming career as a jurist through the guidance of a local Shāfiʿite scholar named Aḥmad al-Radhkānī, Ghazālī joined the circle of the most eminent exponent of Sufism in Ṭūs, Yūsuf al-Nassāj. The great worth of Nassāj's mystical science to Ghazālī became speedily evident by releasing the young genius from an acute intellectual and spiritual torment for which Radhkānī's jurisprudence could have no possible answer.

The first-person account of this interlude, generally dated to his teenage years *circa* 468/1075, is given by Ghazālī in his late autobiographical work, *al-Munqidh min al-ḍalāl* (*The Deliverer from Error*). He speaks to begin with of his loss of belief in received religious truths or dogmas (*taqlīdiyāt*). In terms which have a remarkably modern resonance, he tells of how as a young man he was struck by the relativity of religious truth, given the diversity of faiths. He cites the famous prophetic Tradition (*ḥadīth*) according to which 'Every child is born endowed with the primordial disposition (*fiṭra*): then his parents make him Jewish, Christian, or Zoroastrian'.[17] The radicalism of Ghazālī's reasoning is somewhat hidden here by his recourse to the Prophet's authority in expressing it. For implicit in the Tradition is that Islam is at one with the 'primordial disposition', that it is the original 'Adamic' faith, and other religions are superimposed on it through enculturation. But by his use of the tradition in this context, Ghazālī unmistakably brackets Islam *itself* with other religions, as widely upheld on the simple basis of childhood indoctrination.

If such grounds were woefully insufficient for Ghazālī to assent to *taqlīdiyāt*, he as yet retained his faith in other channels of knowledge, namely sense data (*maḥsūsāt*) and the 'necessary' truths of reason (*ʿaqliyāt* or *ḍarūriyāt*) such as mathematical and logical truths. However, through an unflinching quest for *absolute* certainty of knowledge,[A] Ghazālī found that even his faith in these channels was not unshakeable. He notes that sight is the most powerful of the sense faculties, yet is clearly contradicted by reason in some cases. Shadows look unmoving, but are rationally known to be in motion insofar as cast by the sun; again, sight shows a celestial body as tiny, which geometry can demonstrate is in fact vast. In such cases sense perception is clearly found wanting by reason. But then reason itself can in turn be justly doubted according to Ghazālī. Using the metaphor of a courtroom drama for this transition to absolute *skepsis*, Ghazālī's condemned senses loudly complain that just

[A]In his own words, he sought knowledge such that 'the very possibility of error and delusion (*wahm*) would not be associated with it'. In more technical terms, Ghazālī's goal was apodictic, rather than problematic knowledge. Ghazālī, *al-Munqidh min al-ḍalāl wa 'l-mūṣil ilā Dhī 'l-ʿizzati wa 'l-jalāl*, p. 11.

as they have been judged liars by the higher faculty of reason, why should there not be found in due course an even higher faculty than reason which similarly establishes the relativity of its claims? The, as yet, unmanifest nature of that new mode of perception does not *per se* prove its impossibility.[A] Moreover, the dream state indicates that the sense of absolute certitude accompanying the 'necessary truths' of reason may in fact be misplaced. For absolute conviction also accompanies the data of dreams—until, that is, the subject awakes.

The collapse of faith in reason brought on a two month period of psychological trauma which Ghazālī freely describes as an illness. For someone who was to become a pillar of the Seljuq religious establishment he is shockingly frank when he admits that at this time he remained a Muslim only verbally (*bi-ḥukmi 'l-nuṭq wa 'l-maqāl*), while inwardly he was a pure sceptic (*ʿalā madhhab al-safsaṭa*).[18] The severity of his condition is only grasped if the hyper-sensitivity of Ghazālī's personality is appreciated. The problem was clearly far more than a cerebral one, an intellectual conundrum.[B] It was inwardly experienced as a fatal disorder, irreversible for the obvious reason that Ghazālī had lost the only obvious means of escape: his own rationality. He could therefore not simply *think* his way out of the abyss. In the end, his ascent from it is presented in mysterious, patently mystical terms. Ghazālī thus says that he prayed like a man at his wits' end to whatever God there might be. And a beatific answer indeed came back to him which he describes as 'a light which God the Exalted hurled into my chest'.[19] Full confidence

[A] *ʿAdamu tajallī dhālika 'l-idrāki lā yadullu ʿalā istiḥālatihi, ibid.*, p. 13. The proposition seems pivotal in finally precipitating Ghazālī's absolute *skepsis*. Compare the dictum 'Absence of evidence is not evidence of absence'.

[B] It is the psychological drama of Ghazālī's scepticism which marks it out within the surprisingly strong sceptical tradition of medieval Islam, represented for instance by Ṣāliḥ ibn ʿAbd al-Quddūs's *Kitāb al-Shukūk*. See Joseph van Ess, 'Skepticism in Islamic Religious Thought', in *Al-Abḥāth* 21 (1968), pp. 1–18.

in the channels of knowledge and equilibrium was thereby restored.

This mysterious resolution is considerably clarified if Ghazālī's crisis is co-ordinated with the famous bout of scepticism undergone over five hundred years later by the French philosopher René Descartes (d. 1650). As presented in his *Meditationes de Prima Philosophia*, Descartes' rather academic exercise (significantly perhaps, dedicated to the doctors of the Sorbonne) lacks the terrible immediacy and fearsome psychological impact of Ghazālī's crisis, though Descartes does once liken the experience to falling into a deep whirlpool.[20] But in other respects Ghazālī's experience of *safsaṭa* and Descartes' 'hyperbolic doubt' are similar enough for scholars to have sought some definite historical influence—so far, arguably in vain.[21]

Thus many of the sceptical moves of the two thinkers are the same, including initially setting aside parental beliefs, proposing mathematical truth as a standard of certainty, the destructive parallel of the dream state, and of course the final dismissal of reason's reliability itself. While much is generally made of Descartes' way of assenting at least to his own existence (on the basis of the Cartesian *cogito*, 'I think therefore I am'), the main key to Descartes' resolution of his doubt is in fact the reinstatement of belief in God. For as he argues in the Fourth Meditation, an omnipotent and omnibenevolent being would not involve him in an absolute deception.[A] Put otherwise, if God exists, the faculty of judgement is supplied with an ultimate guarantee. This then is surely also the consideration ellipted by Ghazālī in his mystifying account of the resolution of his crisis. If only his faith in God could be rediscovered, He would represent the ultimate guarantor for all those ways of knowing which had fallen to his total *skepsis*. Descartes for his part dedicates the whole Third Meditation to developing ingenious arguments for God's existence, and these arguments

[A]'I recognize that it is impossible that God should ever deceive me...' Descartes, *Meditations*, p. 37.

are broadly ontological in complexion (i.e. purely *a priori* and concept-based) for the obvious reason that Descartes, like Ghazālī, had lost confidence in the external world shown by the senses, which might have formed alternative grounds for concluding God's existence.

But it has been pointed out that merely relinquishing these extra-mental grounds for restoring his faith in God is not enough for Descartes. To recall, Descartes, just like Ghazālī, had fallen into doubt about reason itself. Yet here he is, ingeniously *using* reason to retrieve his theism—an impasse which remains one of the most notorious and intractable problems in Descartes' philosophy, under the heading of the 'Cartesian circle'. Ghazālī's genius lies in wholly escaping this vicious circularity. For Ghazālī's primary evidence for God is not *per se* rational at all, but a supposedly immediate, supra-rational encounter with Him born of prayer. It is certainly historically significant that while the main harbinger of modern thought could never honestly escape the vortex of his scepticism due to his self-imposed confinement by rationality, the figurehead of traditional Islam instead grounds his own, in practice, remarkably developed rationality (and by extension that of his whole civilization) in an ultimately mystical perception of God, best known under its Sufi name, as *dhawq* ('direct tasting', 'personal experience').[A]

While a mystical experience saved Ghazālī's faith and sanity at this crucial point, formal Sufism as yet vied with other disciplines for his attention. He was earmarked for the career of a high-flying religious scholar and made his way to the

[A]The exceptionality of such perception goes against comparing it with the Augustinian theory of 'divine illumination', later championed in medieval Europe by the Franciscans in the 13th century—a cognitive theory proposing divine intervention in even the most routine activity of the intellect. See R. Pasnau, 'Henry of Ghent and the Twilight of Divine Illumination'. Ghazālī's concept instead closely corresponds with the experience of divine 'effulgence' (*eklampsis*) explored in the mystical theology of the Eastern Church, and especially Gregory Palamas (d. 1359).

greatest intellectual centre of eastern Islam, Nīshāpūr, where he studied with the eminent Ashʿarī theologian Abū 'l-Maʿālī ʿAbd al-Malik ibn Muḥammad al-Juwaynī (d. 478/1085), known as *Imām al-Ḥaramayn*. While a student in Nīshāpūr, Ghazālī also attended the circle of the important contemporary Sufi Abū ʿAlī al-Farmadhī, a direct disciple of the most eminent name of Sufi thought in the early Seljuq period, Abū 'l-Qāsim al-Qushayrī (d. 465/1072). With their distinctive concern for Ashʿarī orthodoxy, Ghazālī and Qushayrī are routinely associated as epitomic Seljuq period Sufi thinkers and their historical linkage through the figure of Farmadhī is correspondingly noteworthy.

A turning point was reached in 484/1091 when Ghazālī visited the military camp (*muʿaskar*) of Niẓām al-Mulk. He had already made a name for himself as an expert scholar and debater and found great favour with the venerable statesman. According to his earliest biographer, ʿAbd al-Ghāfir al-Fārisī, Ghazālī was given in succession the pre-eminent rank of 'Imām of Khorāsān' and 'Imām of Iraq', and was quickly sent by Niẓām al-Mulk to take over as the head of his Niẓāmiyya college in Baghdad.[22] While in the caliphal capital, Ghazālī (still in his early thirties) plunged into a heavy routine of lecturing and writing. From this period date the works which established his name as the paragon and greatest spokesman of Sunnī orthodoxy, notably his monumental attack on Ibn Sīnā's philosophical theology, *Tahāfut al-falāsifa*. His refutation of Ismāʿīlism should also be mentioned, *Faḍā'iḥ al-Bāṭiniyya*. The latter was commissioned by the ʿAbbāsid Caliph himself, al-Mustaẓhir bi-'Llāh (*reg.* 478/1094–512/1118),[23] doubtless in the wake of the assassination in 485/1092 of Niẓām al-Mulk, supposedly by a Nizārī Ismāʿīlī *fidā'ī*.[24]

Yet the hostility voiced in these works should not be taken at absolutely face value. Ghazālī gives a threefold categorization of his teachings in his *Mīzān al-ʿamal*: transmitted dogmas maintained through communal partisanship (*taʿaṣṣub*) in public contexts such as debates; teachings shared to a greater or lesser degree with disciples; and finally doctrines secretly believed to be the truth, shared only with others with the same level of understanding.[A] This tripartite ranking of teachings into exoteric, discipular and esoteric ones, is critical in weighing Ghazālī's views.[B]

In the overall context of this tiered approach to truth, the deepest dynamic of Ghazālī's thought is found to be assimilative. In the *Munqidh* he gives prominence to the saying of ʿAlī ibn Abī Ṭālib, 'Do not recognize the truth through men, but recognize the truth and thereby recognize its partisans'.[25] He is, in other words, wholly uninterested in intellectual partisanship for its own sake and his concern is always with validity and intellectual merit wherever it may be found. He thus rarely rejects a school's teachings outright. Rather, at the exoteric level he fiercely suppresses whatever in them he deems at odds with the formal norms of *religio revelata*, but as the esoteric level of his thought is approached (via the discipular) elements of these very doctrines are absorbed and enrich his thinking. The broad trend is thus to rescue insights from 'heretical' contexts and integrate them into a totalized Islam.

Ghazālī's notorious attack on Ibn Sīnā's philosophy is a case in point. A gathering tide of scholarship has laid bare the profoundly philosophical tenor of Ghazālī's deeper perspective

[A] *Al-madhhab ismun mushtarikun li-thalāthi marātiba iḥdāhā mā yataʿaṣṣabu lahu fi 'l-mubāhāt wa 'l-munāẓarāt wa 'l-ukhrā mā yasīru bihi fi 'l-taʿlīmāt wa 'l-irshādāt wa 'l-thālithatu mā yaʿtaqiduhu 'l-insānu fī nafsihi mimmā 'nkashafa lahu min al-naẓariyāt wa-li-kulli kāmilin thalāthatu madhāhiba bi-hādha 'l-iʿtibār*, Ghazālī, *Mīzān al-ʿamal*, p. 406.

[B] These degrees are co-ordinated by Watt with another threefold hierarchy presented by Ghazālī: 'servile imitation' (*taqlīd*), 'knowledge' (*ʿilm*) and 'tasting/personal experience' (*dhawq*). W. M. Watt, 'A Forgery in al-Ghazālī's *Mishkāt*?', in *Journal of the Royal Asiatic Society*, pp. 18–20. Hava Lazarus-Yafeh's denial of the existence of a Ghazālian esoterism is all the more bewildering, given that it comes after her presentation of this data from the *Mīzān*, as well as a quotation from *al-Maqṣad al-asnā* to the effect that the statement of the authentic truth (*kunh al-ḥaqq*) is almost the opposite (*yakādu yukhālifu*) of what the masses have supposed. H. Lazarus-Yafeh, *Studies in al-Ghazzali*, p. 362.

and higher theology, in which Ibn Sīnā's influence is palpable.[26] This influence was in fact noted long ago: Ibn Taymiyya (d. 728/1328) was not alone amongst medieval critics of the 'Proof of Islam' in decrying his Avicennan tendency.[A] Ibn al-Jawzī (597/1200) went so far as to impute to him some trace of Ismāʿīlī 'Bāṭinī' ideas.[B] While this is obviously a bid to defame Ghazālī, it is also surprisingly the view reached by some recent scholars.[27] Ghazālī's assimilative bent is perhaps even clear in his counter-heretical writing itself, for he characteristically adopts the conceptual framework of the very groups he is arguing with. Thus his attack on Ibn Sīnā is essentially philosophical, and claims to criticize his unscriptural teachings on purely rational grounds. Again, his involved arguments against Ismāʿīlism, while vehemently critical in tone, nevertheless adopt its central premise that 'authoritative instruction' (*taʿlīm*) is absolutely necessary.[C]

Discontent with narrowly externalist and dogmatic considerations is above all behind the second personal crisis which engulfed Ghazālī from the beginning of 488/1095, the painful first-hand account of which is again given in the *Munqidh*. He speaks of how, in shouldering his busy and highly visible role in Baghdad, his level of engrossment in worldly life began to dawn on him. The best of what he did he took to be teaching subjects like jurisprudence and scholastic theology at the Niẓāmiyya, but these now struck him as being sciences ultimately 'unimportant and useless in the pilgrimage to the Hereafter'.[D] Above all he observed his own motives in his meteoric

[A] Ibn Taymiyya says that Ghazālī's esoteric books (*al-kutub al-maḍnūn bi-hā ʿalā ghayr ahli-hā*) have a purely philosophical content, deriving from Ibn Sīnā (*hiya falsafa maḥḍa salaka fīhā maslaka Ibn Sīnā*). Ibn Taymiyya, *Kitāb al-Nubuwwāt*, p. 82.

[B] . . . *Wa hādhā min jinsi kalāmi 'l-Bāṭiniyya*. Ibn al-Jawzī, *Talbīs Iblīs*, p. 180.

[C] 'What is correct [in debating with the Ismāʿīlīs] is to acknowledge the need for an authoritative instructor (*muʿallim*) and that he must be an infallible instructor'. Ghazālī, *Munqidh*, p. 29.

[D] . . . *ʿUlūm ghayr muhimma wa-lā nāfiʿa fī ṭarīq al-ākhira*. Ghazālī, *Munqidh*, p. 36.

career and found them profoundly egoistic and vain. A gathering awareness that divine judgement and final salvation pertained to the individual's inner reality, not the mask of public repute and behaviour, terrified Ghazālī: 'I became certain that I was on the brink of a crumbling bank and already on the verge of falling into hellfire.'[28] He suffered what would now be called a nervous breakdown, referring to a sudden incapacity to speak publicly with the clinical symptoms of aphasia and wholesale loss of appetite. The psychological collapse unfolded over a six month period and was only resolved by a total change of direction. Consoling himself with the knowledge that his family would be well supported through an efficient system of religious endowments, he left everything behind. Under the pretext of fulfilling the Greater Pilgrimage (*Ḥajj*), Ghazālī embraced the anonymous way of life of the dervish, the wandering Muslim *religieux*, and headed for Syria where it is said he intended to become the disciple of the great contemporary Sufi master, Naṣr al-Maqdisī. In Damascus he gave himself up (in his own words) to 'seclusion and retreat (*khalwa*), spiritual exertion (*riyāḍa*) and struggle, devoting myself to the purification of my soul, cultivating virtues and cleansing my heart for the remembrance of God the Exalted, as I had learnt from the Sufis' writings.'[29]

While dramatic conversion and renunciation is a *topos* of Sufi hagiography,[30] speaking of Ghazālī's second crisis as a crux in the intellectual history of medieval Islam would not be hyperbole. The crisis stands for the private discovery by the greatest intellectual mouthpiece for resurgent Sunnism under the Seljuqs, that without the dimension of spirituality, constituted in practice by Sufism, the religion remained a dead letter. Ghazālī moreover dedicated the rest of his intellectual career to putting Sufism at the centre of Islam. The main vehicle for this was his *magnum opus*, the 'Revival of the Religious Sciences' (*Iḥyā' ʿulūm al-dīn*) in which the spiritualization of the religion was discussed from every point of view. In large parts of the Sunnī world the work has retained its enormous authority and popularity till today and was even modified for a

Twelver Shīʿī readership in the Ṣafavid period by Mullā Muḥsin Fayḍ Kāshānī (d. 1091/1680).

In the *Iḥyāʾ*, then, Ghazālī generalizes from his own trauma and seeks to revive Islam at large through its mystical dimension. The basic aim was to counter insincerity through systematically internalising the religion, and on these grounds Ghazālī makes the astonishing ruling in *Ayyuhā ʾl-walad* that the science of the states of the heart (*ʿilm aḥwāl al-qalb*, a euphemism for Sufism) is an individual obligation, not just a collective one.[A] The bid to steep the community at large in Sufi spirituality was outwardly successful beyond all expectation, largely through the pervasion of organized orders (sing. *ṭarīqa*, pl. *ṭuruq*) in the period after the Seljuqs.

Yet his ultimate thinking in championing Sufism is even more radical than this. A close reading of the later part of the section on 'The Ways of the Sufis' (*Ṭuruq al-Ṣūfiyya*) in the *Munqidh* lays bare a yet deeper stratum of thinking. It suggests that Ghazālī in part attributed his own insincerity in practising Islam to lingering uncertainty about the reality of prophethood. Heartfelt assent to religion would only come via certainty in the faculty through which religion is in the first place delivered, namely, prophecy. In other words, a crisis which *prima facie* sprang from a problem of religious ethics was diagnosed by Ghazālī as rooted in an even deeper issue of epistemology. Thus *both* of Ghazālī's crises in fact turn out to pertain to problems of epistemology. The sheer daring of the function Ghazālī assigns to Sufism only now fully comes to light. For he states quite clearly that direct personal evidence of the reality of the prophetic faculty is actually provided through the practice of Sufism. Indeed, his assertion is that amongst Muslims *only* the Sufis really understand the prophetic faculty: 'Whoever is not granted anything of [the attainments of the Sufis] by way of "tasting", grasps nothing of the reality

[A] It is, in other words, a responsibility for every adult Muslim (*farḍ ʿayn*), according to capacity, and not a responsibility left to specially qualified individuals within the community (*farḍ al-kifāya*). See p. 58.

of prophecy save the name'.[31] He is of course cautious in maintaining the unique and foreclosed status of prophecy by immediately stating that the mystical attainments of the Sufis only correspond with the threshold, the very earliest states, of the prophets (*karāmāt al-awliyā' bidāyāt al-anbiyā'*). Ghazālī's careful comparison is with the Prophet Muḥammad's condition just *before* the beginning of the cycle of divine revelation, when he was given to deep communion with God in the cave of Ḥirā'.[32] Yet the message remains unequivocal: Sufism provides certain privileged individuals with direct proof that prophecy is possible, and the continuing presence of such individuals in the midst of Muslim society amounts to a second-hand but invaluable on-going evidence for the faithful.[A]

Despite the obvious boldness of this view of Sufism, Ghazālī's dedication to the moral good of the wider community and the benefit of the common believer is still to the fore here. While key texts prove Ghazālī's commitment to the highest arcana and doctrines of Sufism, his mysticism is distinctive in ultimately sub-serving the renewal of Muslim society in general and is not simply autotelic. This is in fact mirrored in his own biography in which the flight from Baghdad and his incommunicado travels proved to be only an interlude heralding the return of a transformed man to society. He thus states that after dwelling in Damascus for nearly two years and then a shorter stay in Jerusalem, he fulfilled the duty of the Greater Pilgrimage in 490/1097,[33] only to be drawn back to the caliphal capital by the 'appeals of his children'. With this his wandering ended—though not his seclusion, which he clung to in some form (by his own testimony) till 499/1106. In the month of Dhū 'l-

[A] 'Whoever is not granted "tasting" may be certain of it through observation and listening to others, if he frequently associates with them, so that he understands that for sure by the evidences of states.' *Munqidh*, p. 40. It is noteworthy that Ghazālī alludes to the function of the Sufi shaykh in *Ayyuhā 'l-walad* in similarly elevated terms, as the very 'representative of God's Messenger' (*nā'ib rasūl Allāh*) and as 'a light from among the lights of the Prophet' (*nūr min anwār al-nabī*). See p. 34 and p. 36.

Qaᶜda/July of that year he bowed to the orders of the Seljuq vizier, Fakhr al-Mulk (son of Niẓām al-Mulk), and belatedly took up a teaching position at the Niẓāmiyya in Nīshāpūr.[34] The re-emergence of Ghazālī as a fully public figure has a primarily symbolic significance because as early as a year later, the great man made a final move to his childhood home of Ṭūs where he set about realizing an ambition to found a Sufi 'monastery' *(khānqāh)*.[A] Here he would die barely four years later aged only fifty-three, leaving behind a contribution whose reverberations continue in Islamic thought till now.

His life experience, moreover, seems to enshrine a compelling message for countless people in the present day, whatever their precise religious background. Such souls perforce inhabit societies in which the bankruptcy of traditional religion is taken for granted, but cannot suppress their profoundly human need for transcendence. Ghazālī seems to confirm that while religion may indeed remain a closed book on the basis of a merely formalistic and dogmatic approach, it can yet be truly rediscovered in all its fullness through its spiritual and mystical dimensions.

III. CONTENT OF *Ayyuhā 'l-walad*

That Ghazālī does not speak elsewhere of '*Letter to a Disciple*' does not entail its inauthenticity but probably simply that it is one of his last works, written in the context of the Ṭūs *khānqāh*.[B] If so, it acquires something of the *pathos* of a spiritual 'last testament'. Ghazālī's silence about it may also bespeak its

[A] Fakhr al-Mulk was assassinated at this time and it may be that Ghazālī felt himself to be released thereby from his new appointment.

[B] As proposed by W. M. Watt, 'The Authenticity of the Works Attributed to al-Ghazālī', pp. 24–25. Watt places *Ayyuhā 'l-walad* along with *al-Munqidh min al-ḍalāl* and *Mishkāt al-anwār* in the very last phase of Ghazālī's life. The criterion he uses is the concept and terminology of *dhawq*, a supra-rational mode of knowledge, notable by its absence in the *Iḥyā'*. In the *Iḥyā'*, Ghazālī is held to equate intuition with reason in a doctrine of Avicennan type. Next come 'later dogmatic works' which clearly come after the *Iḥyā'* because

originally private nature, despite its later popularity. Its personal and essentialized approach brings us face to face with Ghazālī as *murshid*—a master of the inner life. According to the preamble, he addresses a disciple who has asked for 'what I need in a few pages to be with me for the rest of my life.'[35] The disciple only wants the absolutely indispensable and quotes the prayer of the Prophet, 'O God, I take refuge in Thee from knowledge which is not useful!'[36]

The hints on the mysterious addressee[A] are confusing. Given the title, *Ayyuhā 'l-walad*, (literally, 'O Son!') many have taken him to be a youth.[B] Yet this seems at odds with the idea in the preamble that he is an advanced scholar (*wāḥid min al-ṭalabati 'l-mutaqaddimīn*) who has dedicated 'the best part of my life' (*rayʿāna ʿumrī*) to study and has served the master in the past.[37] There is also an argument for the relative maturity of the disciple in his specifically inquiring about *dhawqī* questions, pertaining to spiritual experience. That said, the individual is probably not yet in middle age. George Hourani has argued that there is evidence for this in Ghazālī's use of a Tradition in the text according to which someone who has reached forty without the good of the soul dominating the evil should prepare for hellfire: 'to say this to a man over forty would be pointless and discouraging.'[38]

The epistolary framework was routine and some have even seen the 'dear friend' or 'brother in religion' addressed in so

they refer to it, but which do not yet propagate *dhawq*. Finally, come the works mentioned, which do explicitly promote it. Watt says that 'there is a high probability that [*Ayyuhā 'l-walad*] is authentic' largely on the basis of the intrinsic compatibility of its contents with Ghazālī's known perspective. *Ibid.*, p. 43.

[A]One of the manuscripts, number 4932 at the Bibliothèque Nationale, Paris (dated 1090/1679), supplies the disciple with a name: ʿAbd Allāh ibn al-Ḥajj Khalīl.

[B]Sabbāgh, for example, translated *Ayyuhā 'l-walad* as *O Jeune Homme!* Scherer gave his 1930 English translation the title 'O Youth', though he admitted the problems of this interpretation. See G. H. Scherer, *O Youth*, note 1, p. 53.

many of Ghazālī's works as a literary expedient.[39] It is moreover clear that the preamble (up to and including the phrase *wa 'Llāhu aʿlam*, 'and God knows best') is an addition post-dating the epistle itself which it introduces in a voice clearly other than Ghazālī's. How firm a basis for contextualization is this information from some later editor? References in the body of the epistle suspiciously speak of an extended list of questions[A] rather than the single question which is actually found in the preamble. At any rate, completely suspending judgement on the historicity of the exchange, it is noticeable that the addressee strikingly resembles Ghazālī himself at a certain age. The text assumes someone given over to disciplines like Kalām theology and jurisprudence, and even contains advice on how to preach to an audience with genuine salutary impact.[40] It is hard to read Ghazālī's counsel to avoid as far as possible the urge to enter into arguments with people[41] or to spurn under any circumstances the tainted benefactions of the ruling class,[42] without recalling the author's own history. Whether the man existed or not, Ghazālī is *in effect* advising himself as he was in his early thirties—a young preacher steeped in exoteric learning, prone to vanity, and quite possibly on course for spiritual disaster.

It is this elusive autobiographical factor which gives *Ayyuhā 'l-walad* its galvanic force and sense of urgency. Even though it probably post-dates it by fifteen years, the epistle's message is ultimately rooted in the bitter experience of the 488/1095 collapse. The text epitomizes Ghazalī's spiritual ethics which were moulded in the furnace of that personal psychological ordeal. This distinctive spirituality, born of crisis as it was, has powerful relevance for the modern reader. In parts, an almost existential sense of life's transience is expressed in the epistle (e.g. 'Live as long as you want, but you must die, love whatever you want, but you will be separated from it. . . ').[43] Early in the text the individual who remains inert in the face of the human

[A]Notably: '. . . As for the rest of your questions, some are covered in my works, so look for them there. And putting others in writing is an offence'. See p. 40.

predicament is compared to someone who is being charged by an angry lion but takes no action.[44] The answer for Ghazālī lies in embracing a spiritual *praxis* while there is opportunity, the Sufi *conversio* (*tawba*) producing a total re-orientation in outlook and lifestyle which transfigures one's existence in this world and conduces to salvation in the next. Ghazālī prescribes this radical therapy with a powerful guarantee, vouching for it on empirical grounds and swearing in God's name to its efficacy on the basis of his own experience: 'O disciple—by God (*bi-'Llāhi*), if you travel [i.e., exert yourself in the spiritual life] you will see marvels at every stage!'[45] Using imagery which remains potent despite familiarity, Ghazālī quotes a Persian couplet to the effect that if you really want 'oblivion' (*shīdā'ī*, literally translated) it is no good just *looking* at the wine.[46] The stress on transformative spiritual action and the promise of actual experience of transcendental reality is as exciting and motivational now as it must have been a millennium ago.

In historical context, *Ayyuhā 'l-walad* presents the salient concepts of Sufi ethics for the specific benefit of a contemporary scholar-preacher—a younger member of the religious class (*ʿulamā'*) on whose high-minded integrity depended the overall spiritual vitality of Islam. In its own way the epistle is thus at the 'cutting edge' of Ghazālī's life project of vitalizing Islam through Sufi spirituality. It is clear that a principal objective of the book is to uproot covert worldliness in the Muslim clergy. For example, at one point Ghazālī asks 'I do not know what the motive was in (learning)—if it was winning the goods of the world, the allure of its vanities, getting its honours, and vainglory to the debit of your associates and peers, woe to you and woe again!'[47] Ghazālī has violent contempt—born of personal acquaintance—for any spokesman for religion who hypocritically fails to implement its real message in his own inner life, and he quotes the prophetic Tradition, 'The man most severely punished on the Day of Resurrection is a scholar whom God did not benefit by his knowledge.'[48] The learned were confronted at the time by a doctrine which seemed specifically to indulge a tendency to self-satisfaction and belief in the sufficiency of cerebral knowledge. This was the teaching of posthumous 'intellectual *eudæmonia*' propounded by Muslim Peripateticism and especially Ibn Sīnā. It is singled out for particular attack by Ghazālī at one point early in the text.[49]

An urgent summons to God-fearing self-exertion consistent with *metanoia* predominates in the epistle, 'let yourself not feel safe from being removed from the corner of your home to the chasm of hellfire.'[50] This sober *ethos*, together with Ghazālī's typical insistence on basic conformity with the Holy Law (*Sharīʿa*), has been mistaken by some scholars to betoken a critical stance on Sufism. For example, G. H. Scherer said in the introduction to Sabbāgh's French translation, 'Dans *Ayyuhā 'l-Walad* il condamne les Soufis pour les excès où ils se laissent entraîner, les caprices de leurs "paroles extatiques" et leurs "cris violents"...'[51] This obviously refers to Ghazālī's statement 'And you must not be deceived (*taghtarra*) by the ecstatic expressions (*shaṭḥ* = 'theopathic utterance') and outbursts of the Sufis.'[52] But while this may be an attack on the Sufi genre of *shaṭḥiyāt* it cannot be a general condemnation of Sufis, as Scherer makes out, because Ghazālī goes on immediately to give a positive definition of their way, '... travel (*sulūk*) on this path should be by way of self-exertion...'[53] A critical view of the genre of *shaṭḥiyāt* would be firmly in the sober 'Junaydī' tradition *within* Sufism. In fact, though Ghazālī does elsewhere look askance on *soi-disant* ecstatics (in terms close to those he employs in this very statement)[54] in his *Mishkāt al-anwār*, he carefully justifies theopathic utterances on the basis of the perspective later known as 'the unity of witnessing' (*waḥdat al-shuhūd*), essentially a doctrine of 'subjective theomonism'.[55] Since his ultimate attitude to *shaṭḥiyāt* is not one of pure dismissal, the verb *ightarra* which he uses here surely means 'be deceived' in the sense of being dazzled rather than simply being taken in by a falsehood. Ghazālī is warning against presumptious identification with the ecstatic aspect of the tradition and misappropriating it to excuse laxity, rather than condemning it *per se*. Sabbāgh's translation of a quotation from Dhū 'l-Nūn al-Miṣrī in the epistle is objectionable on like grounds. For the sentence *in qadarta ʿalā badhli 'l-rūḥi fa-taʿālā wa-illā fa-lā tashtaghil bi-turrahāti 'l-Ṣūfiyya* Sabbāgh translates 'Si tu peux donner ta vie, viens à moi; sinon ne t'occupes pas des futilités du Soufisme.'[56] Rendering *turrahāt al-Ṣūfiyya* as 'futilités du Soufisme' makes Dhū 'l-Nūn—one of the greatest Sufis of all time—an apparent critic of Sufism. *Turrahāt* is better translated here as 'travesties', so that the statement amounts to a condemnation of the appropriation of Sufism by the unworthy, not a condemnation of Sufism *per se*.

In reality *Ayyuhā 'l-walad* is fundamentally Sufi. This is clear for example in its citation of known mystical authorities, its insistence on the master-disciple framework and discussion of its proprieties (*adab*), the technical terminology of spiritual journeying (*sulūk*), mystical states (*aḥwāl*), direct experience (*dhawq*), its anti-formalism and quietism, and its insistence that any non-theocentric motivation whatsoever is futile. In passing, reference is made to gnosis, '. . . unless you kill the ego with sincere exertion your heart will not be animated by the lights of gnosis (*anwār al-maʿrifa*).'[57] The central importance of such a formulation might easily be missed. It is in reality of asymmetric value in correctly gauging the overall purgative accent of the epistle and of Ghazālī's spiritual ethics in general. The call to give the ego death, thereby to give the heart life through gnosis, is a profound key to Ghazālī's spirituality, encountered regularly in his works in different forms.[A] It shows that it is simply false that the gnostic vertex of Ghazālī's worldview bears no relation to its ethical base, as if bracketed off in a purely separate sphere of understanding. On the contrary, the epiphany of God in the heart of the mystic is directly proportional to

[A]E.g. 'The objective of [the Sufis'] sciences is amputating the obstructions of the ego (*ʿaqabāt al-nafs*), and transcending its blameworthy characteristics and bad attributes, to attain thereby the voiding of the heart from other than God and the beautification of it with the recollection of God (*dhikr Allāh*).' Ghazālī, *Munqidh*, p. 35.

the latter's suppression of the 'idolatry' of ego-consciousness and the veil of quotidian existence, as the Gospel confirms, '*. . . strait is the gate, and narrow is the way, which leadeth unto life, and few there be that find it.*'[58] From the higher Ghazālian point of view the purgative and unitive ways are as seamlessly related as the two halves of the Islamic testimony of faith 'no god but God' (*lā ilāha illa 'Llāh*)—the purgative corresponding with the negation (*nafī*), 'no god', and the unitive corresponding with the affirmation (*ithbāt*), 'but God'. Thus despite Ghazālī's tiered hermeneutic, his spirituality has powerful unity. There is (so to speak) gnosis in his *askēsis*, though this is generally kept in the background. The purgative atmosphere of *Ayyuhā 'l-walad* must ultimately be contextualized along these lines.

The epistle's style fits Ghazālī's aim of impressing the basics of the Sufi ethos on a wider audience. It is significant that throughout, he couches what he says in terms of an authoritative tradition, presenting himself mainly as a quoter and transmitter. His very opening gambit is indeed that all advice worthy of the name should primarily derive from the Qur'ān and the Prophet.[59] Much teaching is given in listed form. Notwithstanding the unmistakable autobiographical backdrop (as already mentioned), his propagation of spiritual values in the epistle is the more effective for being couched impersonally in this way. Ghazālī's message is also greatly aided by his aptitude as a wordsmith. There is, for example, his typical use of rhyming prose (*sajʿ*) at climactic moments or in hammering home an idea. The ingenuity in the details of such formulations is easily missed and hard to render, as the following may show. 'Knowledge without action is madness and action without knowledge is void' renders *al-ʿilmu bi-lā ʿamalin junūn wa 'l-ʿamalu bi-ghayri ʿilmin lā yakūn.*[60] It would be artificial to try to capture in English the totality of the effect of such an expression. Aside from the rhyme here, there is paronomasia, with the metathetic interplay of *lām* and *mīm* in *ʿilm* and *ʿamal*, and there is additionally an elegant chiasmus in how these words are arranged between the two halves of the formulation (*ʿilm*, *ʿamal*: *ʿamal*, *ʿilm*). Almost inevitably, from all of this *only* chiasmus survives in the English.

Against such an example, the epistle never gives the impression of being studiedly rhetorical and Ghazālī in fact strongly advises against wordiness in his guidelines for preaching towards the end of the text. In a brilliant image, he likens the situation to someone who delivers a ventose speech to people whose home is about to be swept away in a flood.[61] Tropes like this abound whose force lies in their simple urgency—such as the already mentioned charging lion. Later Ghazālī familiarly equates spiritual problems with physical sickness and the religious authority's role with the doctor's.[62] At another point the *murshid*'s task is compared to the farmer's, weeding his crop to perfect his harvest.[63] The agricultural metaphor recurs when envy's impact on the aspirant is likened to that of fire on a harvest—ripping through all that has been carefully grown and turning it to charred debris.[64] If the power of such imagery is commensurate with its earthiness, not all the symbols are of this homely sort. Ghazālī in passing transmits (from Abū Bakr al-Ṣiddīq) the potently evocative metaphor of the righteous soul as a bird of Paradise—though now caged, in time to come this bird will roost on the highest towers in the Garden of God.[65] There is wry humour too, as in the reference to the impotent man who absurdly believes that he can understand sexual ecstasy without experiencing it (his friend replies: 'now I know you are impotent *and* stupid').[66] But this is not *just* a joke. Sexual experience has always been taken as a close analogue of spiritual experience and the comparison captures well the absolute inequality of verbal allusion and first hand knowledge.

The epistle at first seems unstructured, with the 'free association' of ideas proper to a one to one discussion. But rationale in the structure is borne out by closer analysis. Firstly, according to the data of the preamble, Ghazālī's most essential spiritual advice is sought. Then the whole first half or so of the epistle is his main response to this: the key to salvation in his view is to take action. At the beginning Ghazālī shows that he especially has in mind members of the learned class who take lazy pride in their knowledge of exoteric science (in due course such disciplines as theology, rhetoric, and grammar are even derided as leading to 'wasting your life in opposition to the Lord of Majesty').[67] The summons to act is naturally initially expressed in the unchallengeable form of a prophetic Tradition,[68] and slightly later through a series of proof texts from the Qur'ān.[69] In the meantime it is also dramatically highlighted by the reported vision of the great Sufi al-Junayd al-Qawārīrī. Having died, Junayd sends word that only secret prayers done by him while others slept carried weight beyond the grave—the ample mystical theorizing for which he was responsible was 'wide of the mark'.[70] The broader message of the need for action shows that Ghazālī simply means hereby to laud Junayd's practice over his speculation, but it is also implied that, of all his religious practices these nightly prayers *alone* had real spiritual impact. In Ghazālī's mouth this cannot really be an antinomian invitation to neglect the Holy Law, but it *is* anti-formalist—the point being that only actions done with concentration and genuine feeling are of account with God. Ghazālī shows no interest in emptily rehearsing rituals as ends in themselves.

The call to earnest action leads directly to a vexing theological question which Ghazālī must get out of the way: what is the exact relationship between works, faith and divine grace? Despite the basically 'hortatory' intent of *Ayyuhā 'l-walad*, subtle doctrinal issues are touched on at this juncture. Muʿtazilism seemingly fits Ghazālī's message of the centrality of action perfectly, with its explicit insistence on attributing salvation to works, which are in turn rooted in the person's objective freedom in acting. But despite his emphasis, Ghazālī here salvages an impeccably Ashʿarī doctrine of *sola gratia*: no-one is actually saved by their deeds as such and he confirms that '. . . the worshipper attains Paradise by the bounty and grace of God (*bi-faḍli 'Llāhi wa-karamihi*).'[71] The antinomy that the believer must act but that salvation is through divine grace is superbly captured in the tradition of ʿAlī ibn Abī Ṭālib, quoted here by

Ghazālī: 'Whoso believes he will attain his goal without effort is a wishful thinker. And whoso believes he will reach his goal by the expending of effort is presumptuous.'[72]

Part of the solution is that virtuous acts are understood by Ghazālī to *predispose* the soul to receive God's grace, on the authority of Qur'ān 7:56: 'The Mercy of God is near to those who do good.'[73] They thus direct the outcome without dictating it. Good acts themselves are anyway technically subordinate to faith. While subordinate, their great significance lies in expressing it and concretizing it. Such is their importance that faith is given an official definition here by Ghazālī which includes righteous acts: faith is not just verbal declaration and intellectual assent (the first 'pillar' of Islam), but it is additionally *action* in accordance with the remaining pillars. Put otherwise: beyond the point of *conversio*, its genuineness is only known from the believer's subsequent good acts which amount to a kind of *conversio continuata*. Thus, after granting faith's predominant role over acts in the individual's getting to Paradise, Ghazālī pointedly asks '... but *when* will he get [to Paradise]? How many difficult obstacles must he overcome before arriving?'[74]

Beyond either faith or works, however, the crowning element in this view of salvation remains divine grace. For instance in a tradition cited from al-Ḥasan al-Baṣrī, God is confirmed as greeting the saved with the words '... enter the Garden *by My Mercy*.' It is not just that grace bears prime responsibility in that God is free to admit or refuse salvation to any soul whatosoever. Ashʿarī necessitarianism dictates that the very presence of faith in the soul was *itself* the result of prevenient grace. In sum: works are indeed indispensable, not in their own right, but as a decisive expression of faith; this then will predispose the soul to become a recipient of the divine grace of salvation; and anyway, prevenient grace was the real origin of the soul's faith and righteous works. Ultimately, God's omnipotence requires that the process of salvation is a circle which begins and ends with the inscrutable mystery of pure grace.

In the above, Ghazālī gives his call to action a theological context. He next transits from generality to specificity and recommends a particular kind of righteous action above others, namely, vigil. As usual, this is done through a variety of proof texts, from prophetic Traditions at the top of the scale of authority, to poetry at the bottom. Next, still on the level of specificity, legal considerations are introduced into the discussion. A vital pre-condition for effective spiritual action is that it must always conform to the revealed Law. Seemingly righteous activity can be wrong if individualistic and at odds with the Sharīʿa. To make his point, Ghazālī picks out stark examples, one of which is fasting on days in the year when this is in fact forbidden.

With the statement in which Ghazālī speaks of gnosis as depending on killing ego consciousness,[75] a pivot is reached in the text which more or less marks the conclusion of the discussion of action *per se*. The passage in question dramatically moves to a more esoteric viewpoint (though it significantly begins with a grave warning against the antinomian misuse of *shaṭḥiyāt*). As before, Ghazālī still derides idle theorising and promotes action, but the reason now given is that certain things are only known through direct tasting (*dhawq*). The only way to communicate these ineffable experiences is to invite the other person to act in the same manner and find out for himself. Thus at the close of his discourse on action Ghazālī has shifted from the consideration of posthumous salvation to the more esoteric one of immanent experience—a clear glimpse, before he moves on, of a vista of altogether higher reaches in his perspective.

The pages which follow are overtly Sufi in complexion. To begin with, there are two stories from the mystics Shiblī and Ḥātim al-Aṣamm respectively. The latter is said to have gained from his master Shaqīq al-Balkhī eight lessons from thirty years of discipleship under him.[76] There follows a list—one of a number characterizing the later part of the epistle. The first four items broadly pertain to the ascetic and otherworldly cultivation of the soul, while the last four mostly pertain to absolute reliance on God. Next, the relationship of spiritual preceptor and disciple is explored.[77] In this, the practical norms of institutional Sufism are unequivocally approved by Ghazālī. The master's function and his appointment of deputies is carefully compared to the Prophet's function as God-sent guide for the Muslim collectivity, and *his* appointment of deputies. The aim here is implicitly to refute any allegation of religious innovation (*bidʿa*). The marks of a person truly eligible to guide in this way, are listed under five headings. The third involves further acknowledgement of the norms of institutional Sufism by Ghazālī: a pre-condition for mastership is that the individual is part of an initiatic chain (*silsila*) returning to the Prophet. Outward and inward veneration of such a guide is enjoined, with specified etiquettes. The definition of Sufism which is next given is simple but highly exacting: correctness of attitude towards God and excellent behaviour with other human beings. The latter is defined as perfecting mildness (*ḥilm*) in interacting with them, and quashing the urge for self-assertion.

Ghazālī by now is going through a list of definitions which have evidently been asked for earlier by the disciple. Definition of technical terms (*iṣṭilāḥāt*) is of course a much used didactic medium in the history of Islamic mysticism. Ghazālī has just defined Sufism and he moves on now to definitions of servanthood (*ʿubūdiyya*), reliance on God (*tawakkul*), and sincerity (*ikhlāṣ*). His definition of the latter is particularly noteworthy as a clear instance of the intrusion of Ashʿarism in Ghazālī's Sufi discourse in the epistle. He suggests as a perfect cure for insincerity or eyeservice (*riyā'*) that one should keep in mind that human beings are nothing but inanimate objects (*jamādāt*), absolutely under God's power. A powerful necessitarianism in fact informs the whole of the epistle.

The epistle's last phase involves a final eightfold list of items of heartfelt advice from the master.[78] Firstly, Ghazālī counsels against arguing. An element of pessimism and quietism colours what he says here, perhaps produced by long experience. Only in one case should one bother to correct ignorance—

that of someone wholly without envy and overestimation of himself, and fundamentally intelligent. But the other three cases of ignorance generally encountered, are hopelessly incurable according to Ghazālī: ignorance involving envy, ignorance involving underestimation of others, and ignorance involving unintelligence. Then as his second item of parting advice, Ghazālī warns about operating as a preacher. So pernicious is the influence of bad preaching that he advocates forcibly removing the person guilty of it as part of the duty of 'commanding the good and forbidding the evil.'[79] The effective preacher must sincerely 'practice what he preaches' and avoid florid and rhetorical verbal displays. There is a glimpse of Ghazālī's first hand knowledge of the spiritual psychology of the masses when he recommends that acquisitive and appetitive instincts should be capitalized on by the skillful preacher, and turned to higher use so that 'acquisitiveness (*ḥirṣ*) and an appetite (*raghba*) for obedience and for repentance from disobedience, will appear.'[80]

The third and fourth items of advice are linked: to avoid politics and royal courts, and to reject the gifts and emoluments of the rulers.[81] This purism was not just to preserve the aspirant's probity, but was surely tied in with Ghazālī's bigger agenda of vitalizing Islam through Sufism. Sufism must stay isolated from the compromising influence of royal and governmental funding which would erode the independent ideals central to its function of spiritual regeneration within society. While the first four items of advice have covered things to be spurned, what follows are things to be positively accomplished: envisage what would delight you in a servant and behave accordingly with God; the message familiar from the Gospels, 'whatsoever ye would that men should do to you, do ye even so to them' (Matthew 7:12);[82] next, to imagine you will only live for another week to get a real perspective on what merits your attention—inessential sciences like jurisprudence and scholastic theology will naturally be replaced by the practice of systematic moral introspection (*murāqabat al-qalb*), central to the Sufi path;[83] finally, to practise pure reliance on God for your needs and never amass wealth.[84]

As requested in the preamble, Ghazālī finally transmits a prayer for the disciple's regular use. The potency of this personal entreaty to God in rhyming prose lies in the way that it confronts the supplicant's crushing sense of unworthiness and reverential fear with hope in the absoluteness of God's mercy. Like other classic examples of powerful supplications in Islam, for example ʿAlī ibn Abī Ṭālib's '*Duʿā Kumayl*', Ghazālī's seems to exploit the disparity between two registers of religious consciousness: on the one hand the ethical register in which the individual is fatally sinful, and on the other the incommensurable onto-theological register in which the Godhead, whose grace is entreated, is the absolute and overwhelming reality. The same point might be expressed in Rudolf Otto's terms as a dynamic tension between the dread proper to the 'element of awefulness'—a consciousness of the just anger of God (*orgê theoû*)—and the pure 'consciousness of creaturehood' pertaining to the element of *majestas*.[85]

IV. ARABIC TEXT OF THE EPISTLE[A]

Bouyges, citing al-Sayyid Murtaḍā,[86] inclines to the view that *Ayyuhā 'l-walad* was originally a Persian work.[B] The problem is complicated and cannot be resolved in this context. Against

[A] A large variety of manuscripts and printed texts of *Ayyuhā 'l-walad* is presented and analysed by Scherer, *O Youth*, pp. 19–32. Scherer's own translation was based on the manuscript he took to be the best among these, Dresden 172, which is fully reproduced in photographs in his volume.

[B] 'Ce recueil d'exhortations morales ou pieuses qui fut, dit-on, écrit d'abord en persan, et qui, traduit en arabe par un anonyme, est devenue celèbre sous le nom de *Ayyuhā 'l-Walad*.' M. Bouyges, *Essai de Chronologie des Œuvres de al-Ghazālī*, p. 60. Note that Scherer also took the epistle to have been originally Persian. Scherer, *O Youth*, note 29, p. 12, also p. 27. More recently Pourjavady has repeated the claim that the epistle derives from a Persian original, *Ay Farzand*. N. Pourjavady, 'Minor Persian Works', in *Encyclopædia Iranica*, vol. x, *s.v.* *Ġazālī*, p. 370.

the thesis of a Persian original is the evidence of two important Persian manuscripts which may be equated with our Arabic text of the epistle: (1) *Resālat-e Ghazālī* = Ms number 1792 from the India Office Library in London; and (2) *Kholāṣat-e taṣānīf Emām Moḥammad Ghazālī dar ʿelm-e solūk* = Ms 14.30 from Berlin. W. Pertsch in his *Die arab Hss. zu Gotha*, clearly describes the Berlin Ms as 'persische Übersetzung.'[87] Moreover H. Ethé in his *Catalogue* describes India Office Ms 1792 as a 'Persian paraphrase' of *Ayyuhā 'l-walad*. Ethé moreover supplies the decisive information that the India Office Ms 1792 is the same in content but different in wording to Berlin 14.30. This observation perhaps suggests that the two Persian manuscripts are separate translations of a common Arabic source and thus that the text is originally Arabic.[88] There is in any case the additional consideration that much in *Ayyuhā 'l-walad* is quoted from other works by Ghazālī which are Arabic, notably the *Iḥyā'*.

The Arabic text presented here as the basis for the translation is derived from the edition of Toufic Sabbagh. The text has been amended slightly by Professor M.A.S. Abdel Haleem to whom warm thanks are due. I would also like to express my sincere gratitude to Juan Acevedo and especially to Fatima Azzam.

Notes to Introduction

[1] E.g. his *al-Mustasfā min ʿilm al-uṣūl*

[2] E.g. his *al-Iqtiṣād fi 'l-iʿtiqād.*

[3] In his *Tahāfut al-falāsifa.* See Ghazālī, *The Incoherence of the Philosophers.*

[4] In his *Faḍā'iḥ al-Bāṭiniyya wa-faḍā'il al-Mustaẓhiriyya.*

[5] J. R. Michot, 'La Pandémie Avicennienne au VIe/XIIe Siècle', *Arabica*, XL (1993), pp. 287–344.

[6] E.g. Ibn Ghaylān al-Balkhī's testimony from the year 523/1129 in Ibn Ghaylān and Ibn Sīnā, *Ḥudūth al-ʿālam and al-Ḥukūmāt*, pp. 10–11. There is also testimony from Shahrastānī (d. 548/1153). See W. Madelung and T. Mayer (ed. and tr.), *Struggling with the Philosopher*, p. 20 (English), p. 3 (Arabic).

[7] See Fazlur Rahman, *Prophecy in Islam: Philosophy and Orthodoxy*, pp. 30–91.

[8] E.g. Ibn Sīnā, *al-Risāla al-aḍḥawiyya fī 'l-maʿād.*

[9] E.g. Ibn Sīnā, *al-Ishārāt wa 'l-tanbīhāt, Namaṭ* 5, *Faṣl* 7, pp. 84–90.

[10] See Paul E. Walker, *Early Philosophical Shiism: The Ismaili Neoplatonism of Abū Yaʿqūb al-Sijistānī.*

[11] See Paul E. Walker, *Ḥamīd al-Dīn al-Kirmānī: Ismaili Thought in the Age of al-Ḥākim.*

[12] See Marshall G. S. Hodgson, *The Order of Assassins.*

[13] See Sara Sviri, 'Ḥakīm Tirmidhī and the Malāmatī Movement in Early Sufism'.

[14] See the abridgement of Massignon's four volume *magnum opus, Hallāj: Mystic and Martyr*, tr. and ed. Herbert Mason.

[15] L. Massignon, *Essay. . .*, p. 189. Also see A. H. Abdel-Kader, *The Life, Personality and Writings of al-Junayd.*

[16] The list would include: *Qūt al-Qulūb* by Abū Ṭālib al-Makkī (d. 386/966), *Kitāb al-Lumaʿ* by Abū Naṣr al-Sarrāj (d. 378/988), *Kitāb al-Taʿarruf* by Abū Bakr al-Kalābādhī (d. *circa* 380/990), *Ṭabaqāt al-Ṣufiyya* by Abū ʿAbd al-Raḥmān al-Sulamī (d. 412/1021), and the only non-Arabic work, *Kashf al-Maḥjūb* by ʿAlī al-Hujwīrī (d. *circa* 464/1071).

[17] Bukhārī, *Janā'iz*, 80, 93.

[18] Ghazālī, *Munqidh*, p. 13.

[19] *Idem.*

[20] At the beginning of the Second Meditation. Descartes, *Meditations on First Philosophy, With Selections from the Objections and Replies*, p. 16.

[21] M. M. Sharif has argued at some length for influence. M. M. Sharif (ed.), *A History of Muslim Philosophy*, vol. 2, p. 1381ff.

[22] Fārisī's biography is translated in R. J. McCarthy, *Freedom and Fulfillment: An Annotated Translation of al-Ghazālī's* Al-Munqidh min al-Ḍalāl, pp. 14–18.

[23] Al-Mustaẓhir's accession indicates the *terminus a quo* of the *Faḍā'iḥ al-Bāṭiniyya*, and its introduction, as well as Ghazālī's *Munqidh*, shows that his commission to refute Ismāʿīlism pre-dates his sudden departure from Baghdad *circa* January 489/1096, which is therefore the *terminus ad quem*.

[24] Some recent scholarship disputes Nizārī responsibility for Niẓām al-Mulk's assassination. See Carole Hillenbrand, '1092: A Murderous Year'.

[25] Ghazālī, *Munqidh*, p. 25.

[26] On Ghazālī's 'philosophical' ethics see M. A. Sherif, *Ghazali's Theory of Virtue*. On the impact of philosophy on his eschatology see T. J. Gianotti, *Al-Ghazālī's Unspeakable Doctrine of the Soul: Unveiling the Esoteric Psychology and Eschatology of the* Iḥyā. On the impact of philosophy on his higher theology see H. Landolt, 'Ghazālī and "Religionswissenschaft"'. On the impact of philosophy on his Ashʿarism see R. Frank, *Al-Ghazālī and the Ashʿarite School.*

[27] F. Jabre, *La Notion de la Certitude selon Ghazālī*, p. 293. H. Lazarus-Yafeh, *Studies in al-Ghazzali*, p. 274. H. Landolt, 'Ghazālī and "Religionswissenschaft"', pp. 43–47.

[28] Ghazālī, *Munqidh*, p. 36, referring to Q. IX: 199.

[29] *Ibid.*, pp. 37–38.

[30] Similar turning points are found for instance with Ibrāhīm ibn Adham (d. 160/777), Fakhr al-Dīn ʿIrāqī (d. 688/1289), ʿAlā' al-Dawla al-Simnānī (d. 736/1336) and Sayyid Ḥaydar Āmulī (8th/14th century).

[31] Ghazālī, *Munqidh*, p. 40.

[32] *Idem.*

[33] *Ibid.*, p. 38.

[34] *Ibid.* p. 49.

[35] See p. 2.

[36] See p. 2.

[37] See p. 2.

[38] G. Hourani, 'The Chronology of Ghazālī's Writings', esp. p. 231.

[39] E.g. R. J. McCarthy, *Freedom and Fulfillment*, note 3, p. 115.

[40] See p. 48.

[41] See p. 42.

[42] See p. 54.

[43] See p. 14.

[44] See p. 8.

[45] See p. 42.

[46] See p. 8.

[47] See p. 14.

[48] See p. 4.

[49] See p. 6.

[50] See p. 18.

[51] Cf. T. Sabbagh, *Lettre au Disciple*, p. xxi.

[52] See p. 24.

[53] See p. 24.

[54] Lazarus-Yafeh, *Studies in al-Ghazzali*, pp. 101–103

[55] Ghazālī, *The Niche of Lights*, p. 18.

[56] Sabbagh, *Lettre au Disciple*, p. 38.

[57] See p. 24.

[58] Matthew 7:14.

[59] See p. 4.

[60] See p. 16.

[61] See p. 50.

[62] See p. 44.

[63] See p. 34.

[64] See p. 46.

[65] See p. 18.

[66] See p. 24.

[67] See p. 14.

[68] See p. 4.

[69] See p. 8.

[70] See p. 6.

[71] See p. 10.

[72] See p. 12.

[73] See p. 10.

[74] See p. 10.

[75] See p. 24.

[76] See p. 28.

[77] See p. 34.

[78] See p. 42.

[79] See p. 52.

[80] See p. 52

[81] See p. 52.

[82] See p. 56.

[83] See p. 56.

[84] See p. 58.

[85] R. Otto, *The Idea of the Holy*, p. 12ff.

[86] Zabīdī, *K. Itḥāf al-sādāt al-muttaqīn bi-sharḥ asrār Iḥyā' ʿulūm al-dīn*, I, 41. 19.

[87] W. Pertsch, *Die arab Hss. zu Gotha*, tome V, p. 25.

[88] But one modern Arabic version of the text is explicitly a translation from Persian. This is the *Kitāb Khulāṣat al-taṣnīf fī 'l-taṣawwuf*, translated into Arabic by Muḥammad Amīn al-Kurdī (d. 1332/1914), evidently from a Persian version identifiable (on the basis of the similarity in titles) with Berlin 14.30.

أيها الولد

In the name of God, the Infinitely Good, the Merciful. Praise belongs to God, the Lord of the worlds, and the 'outcome belongs to the God-conscious,'[1] and blessings and peace be upon His Prophet Muḥammad, and all his family.

Know that one of the advanced students devoted himself to the service of the master, the Imām, the Ornament of Religion and Proof of Islam, Abū Ḥāmid ibn Muḥammad al-Ghazālī (may God sanctify his spirit) and occupied himself with the acquisition and study of knowledge under him, until he mastered the details of the sciences and filled out the good qualities of the soul. Then one day he considered his situation, and it occurred to him, 'I have studied various kinds of science, and I have spent my life learning and mastering them. I now ought to find out which kind will be of use to me on the morrow, to keep me company in my grave, and those which are not of use to me, so that I may give them up. As God's Messenger (God bless him and give him peace) said, 'O God, I take refuge in Thee from knowledge which is not useful!'[2]

This thought persisted to the point that he wrote to the honourable master, the Proof of Islam, Muḥammad al-Ghazālī (may God the Exalted be merciful to him), seeking a ruling, asking questions, and requesting both advice and a prayer, 'Even though the works of the master such as *The Revival* [*of the Religious Sciences* (Iḥyā' ʿulūm al-dīn)] and others contain the answers to my questions, what I want is for the master to write down what I need in a few pages to be with me for the rest of my life, and I will act in accordance with what is in them during my term, if God the Exalted wills.' So the master wrote him this message in reply, and God knows best.

أيها الولد

بِسْمِ ٱللهِ ٱلرَّحْمٰنِ ٱلرَّحِيمِ. اَلْحَمْدُ لِلّٰهِ رَبِّ ٱلْعَالَمِينَ. وَٱلْعَاقِبَةُ لِلْمُتَّقِينَ. وَٱلصَّلَاةُ وَٱلسَّلَامُ عَلَى نَبِيِّهِ مُحَمَّدٍ وَآلِهِ أَجْمَعِينَ.

إِعْلَمْ أَنَّ وَاحِداً مِنَ ٱلطَّلَبَةِ ٱلْمُتَقَدِّمِينَ لَازَمَ خِدْمَةَ ٱلشَّيْخِ ٱلْإِمَامِ زَيْنِ ٱلدِّينِ حُجَّةِ ٱلْإِسْلَامِ أَبِي حَامِدِ بْنِ مُحَمَّدٍ ٱلْغَزَالِيِّ، قَدَّسَ ٱللهُ رُوحَهُ، وَٱشْتَغَلَ بِٱلتَّحْصِيلِ وَقِرَاءَةِ ٱلْعِلْمِ عَلَيْهِ حَتَّى جَمَعَ دَقَائِقَ ٱلْعُلُومِ وَٱسْتَكْمَلَ فَضَائِلَ ٱلنَّفْسِ. ثُمَّ إِنَّهُ تَفَكَّرَ يَوْماً فِي حَالِ نَفْسِهِ وَخَطَرَ عَلَى بَالِهِ وَقَالَ: إِنِّي قَرَأْتُ أَنْوَاعاً مِنَ ٱلْعُلُومِ وَصَرَفْتُ رَيْعَانَ عُمْرِي عَلَى تَعَلُّمِهَا وَجَمْعِهَا، وَٱلْآنَ يَنْبَغِي لِي أَنْ أَعْلَمَ أَيُّ نَوْعِهَا يَنْفَعُنِي غَداً وَيُؤْنِسُنِي فِي قَبْرِي؟ وَأَيُّهَا لَا يَنْفَعُنِي حَتَّى أَتْرُكَهُ، كَمَا قَالَ رَسُولُ ٱللهِ، صَلَّى ٱللهُ عَلَيْهِ وَسَلَّمَ: اَللّٰهُمَّ أَعُوذُ بِكَ مِنْ عِلْمٍ لَا يَنْفَعُ.

فَٱسْتَمَرَّتْ هٰذِهِ ٱلْفِكْرَةُ حَتَّى كَتَبَ إِلَى حَضْرَةِ ٱلشَّيْخِ حُجَّةِ ٱلْإِسْلَامِ مُحَمَّدٍ ٱلْغَزَالِيِّ، رَحِمَهُ ٱللهُ تَعَالَى، ٱسْتِفْتَاءً وَسَأَلَهُ مَسَائِلَ وَٱلْتَمَسَ نَصِيحَةً وَدُعَاءً. قَالَ: وَإِنْ كَانَ مُصَنَّفَاتُ ٱلشَّيْخِ كَٱلْإِحْيَاءِ وَغَيْرِهِ تَشْتَمِلُ عَلَى جَوَابِ مَسَائِلِي، لٰكِنَّ مَقْصُودِي أَنْ يَكْتُبَ ٱلشَّيْخُ حَاجَتِي فِي وَرَقَاتٍ تَكُونُ مَعِي مُدَّةَ حَيَاتِي وَأَعْمَلُ بِمَا فِيهَا مُدَّةَ عُمْرِي، إِنْ شَاءَ ٱللهُ تَعَالَى. فَكَتَبَ ٱلشَّيْخُ هٰذِهِ ٱلرِّسَالَةَ إِلَيْهِ فِي جَوَابِهِ. وَٱللهُ أَعْلَمُ.

'Know O beloved and precious disciple—may God prolong your days in obedience to Him and travel with you on the path of those He loves—that public advice should be quoted from the goldmine of messengerhood [the Prophet]. If you have received advice from him, what need do you have of my advice? And if you have not received it, then tell me what you have achieved in these years gone-by!

أيها الولد

O disciple, included in what God's Messenger (God bless him and give him peace) advised his community, is his statement, 'An indication of the withdrawal of God the Exalted from the worshipper is his busying himself with what does not concern him, and if an hour of a man's life slips by in other than that for which he was created in the way of worship, then it is proper that his affliction be protracted. Whoever passes forty without his virtue overpowering his vice, let him get ready for hellfire!'[3] This advice contains enough for people of knowledge.

أيها الولد

إِعْلَمْ أَيُّهَا ٱلْوَلَدُ ٱلْمُحِبُّ ٱلْعَزِيزُ، أَطَالَ ٱللّٰهُ بَقَاكَ بِطَاعَتِهِ وَسَلَكَ بِكَ سَبِيلَ أَحِبَّائِهِ، أَنَّ مَنْشُورَ ٱلنَّصِيحَةِ يُكْتَبُ مِنْ مَعْدِنِ ٱلرِّسَالَةِ، إِنْ كَانَ قَدْ بَلَغَكَ مِنْهُ نَصِيحَةٌ، فَأَيُّ حَاجَةٍ لَكَ فِي نَصِيحَتِي، وَإِنْ لَمْ يَبْلُغْكَ فَقُلْ لِي مَاذَا حَصَّلْتَ فِي هٰذِهِ ٱلسِّنِينَ ٱلْمَاضِيَةِ؟

أَيُّهَا ٱلْوَلَدُ

أَيُّهَا ٱلْوَلَدُ، مِنْ جُمْلَةِ مَا نَصَحَ بِهِ رَسُولُ ٱللّٰهِ، صَلَّى ٱللّٰهُ عَلَيْهِ وَسَلَّمَ، أُمَّتَهُ قَوْلُهُ، عَلَيْهِ ٱلسَّلَامُ: عَلَامَةُ إِعْرَاضِ ٱللّٰهِ تَعَالَى عَنِ ٱلْعَبْدِ ٱشْتِغَالُهُ بِمَا لَا يَعْنِيهِ، وَإِنْ إِمْرَأً ذَهَبَتْ سَاعَةٌ مِنْ عُمُرِهِ فِي غَيْرِ مَا خُلِقَ لَهُ مِنَ ٱلْعِبَادَةِ، لَجَدِيرٌ أَنْ تَطُولَ عَلَيْهِ حَسْرَتُهُ. وَمَنْ جَاوَزَ ٱلْأَرْبَعِينَ وَلَمْ يَغْلِبْ خَيْرُهُ عَلَى شَرِّهِ فَلْيَتَجَهَّزْ إِلَى ٱلنَّارِ. وَفِي هٰذِهِ ٱلنَّصِيحَةِ كِفَايَةٌ لِأَهْلِ ٱلْعِلْمِ.

أَيُّهَا ٱلْوَلَدُ

O disciple, advice is easy—what is difficult is accepting it, for it is bitter in taste to those who pursue vain pleasures, since forbidden things are dear to their hearts. [This is] particularly so for whoever is the student of conventional knowledge, who is occupied with gratifying his ego and with worldly exploits, for he supposes that his knowledge alone will be his salvation and that his deliverance is in it, and that he can do without deeds—and this is the conviction of the philosophers.[A] Glory be to God Almighty! This conceited fool does not know that when he acquires knowledge, if he does not act on the strength of it, the evidence against him will become decisive, as the Messenger of God (God bless him and give him peace) said, 'The man most severely punished on the Day of Resurrection is a scholar whom God did not benefit by his knowledge.'[4]

It is reported that al-Junayd (may God sanctify his heart) was seen in sleep after he had died, and was asked, 'What is the news Abū 'l-Qāsim?' He said, 'Those expressions were wide of the mark, and those counsels came to nothing. Nothing was of benefit to me except some small prayers I made in the middle of the night.'[5]

أيها الولد

[A]This statement shows that in this section Ghazālī is not just generally attacking the self-satisfaction of the learned, but a definite doctrine of the philosophers: evidently the Neoplatonic teaching that posthumous salvation is attained through the development of the individual's intellectual potentialities while on earth, ultimately producing 'contact' (*ittiṣāl*) with the active intellect. This was held for example by Avicenna (d. 428 AH/1037 CE). The doctrine has been described as follows, 'The soul enjoying supreme *eudæmonia* (*saʿāda*) is the one that achieves a perfect disposition for intellectual thought in the present life.' (H. A. Davidson, *Alfarabi, Avicenna, and Averroes, on Intellect*, OUP, 1992, p. 109). Avicenna, like Fārābī, allegorizes hellfire along the same lines. Since the active intellect is the locus of *eudæmonia*, the souls of those who in life have been fixated with their bodies experience great pain after death.

أَيُّهَا ٱلْوَلَدُ، اَلنَّصِيحَةُ سَهْلَةٌ وَٱلْمُشْكِلُ قَبُولُهَا، لِأَنَّهَا فِي مَذَاقِ مُتَّبِعِي ٱلْهَوَى مُرَّةٌ، إِذْ ٱلْمَنَاهِي مَحْبُوبَةٌ فِي قُلُوبِهِمْ، وَعَلَى ٱلْخُصُوصِ لِمَنْ كَانَ طَالِبَ ٱلْعِلْمِ ٱلرَّسْمِيِّ وَمُشْتَغِلاً فِي فَضْلِ ٱلنَّفْسِ وَمَنَاقِبِ ٱلدُّنْيَا، فَإِنَّهُ يَحْسَبُ أَنَّ ٱلْعِلْمَ ٱلْمُجَرَّدَ لَهُ سَيَكُونُ نَجَاتُهُ وَخَلَاصُهُ فِيهِ وَأَنَّهُ مُسْتَغْنٍ عَنِ ٱلْعَمَلِ. وَهٰذَا ٱعْتِقَادُ ٱلْفَلَاسِفَةِ. سُبْحَانَ ٱللهِ ٱلْعَظِيمِ. لَا يَعْلَمُ هٰذَا ٱلْمَغْرُورُ أَنَّهُ حِينَ حَصَّلَ ٱلْعِلْمَ، إِذَا لَمْ يَعْمَلْ بِهِ، تَكُونُ ٱلْحُجَّةُ عَلَيْهِ آكَدَ كَمَا قَالَ رَسُولُ ٱللهِ، صَلَّى ٱللهُ عَلَيْهِ وَسَلَّمَ: أَشَدُّ ٱلنَّاسِ عَذَاباً يَوْمَ ٱلْقِيَامَةِ عَالِمٌ لَا يَنْفَعُهُ ٱللهُ بِعِلْمِهِ.

وَرُوِيَ أَنَّ ٱلْجُنَيْدَ، قَدَّسَ ٱللهُ سِرَّهُ، رُؤِيَ فِي ٱلْمَنَامِ بَعْدَ مَوْتِهِ فَقِيلَ لَهُ: مَا ٱلْخَبَرُ يَا أَبَا ٱلْقَاسِمِ؟ قَالَ: طَاحَتْ تِلْكَ ٱلْعِبَارَاتُ وَفَنِيَتْ تِلْكَ ٱلْإِشَارَاتُ وَمَا نَفَعَنَا إِلَّا رُكَيْعَاتٌ رَكَعْنَاهَا فِي جَوْفِ ٱللَّيْلِ.

O disciple, be neither destitute of good deeds nor devoid of spiritual states, for you can be sure that mere knowledge will not help. It is as though a man in the desert had ten Indian swords and other weapons besides—the man being brave and a warrior—and a huge, terrifying lion attacked him. What is your opinion? Will the weapons repel this danger of his from him without their being used and being wielded? It is obvious they will not repel it unless drawn and wielded!

Likewise, if a man studied a hundred thousand intellectual issues and understood them, but did not act on the strength of them, they would not be of use to him except by taking action. Or it is as though a man had a temperature and jaundice, which is treated by oxymel and barley infusion—no recovery will take place except by using them.

Though thou pour two thousand measures of wine,
Unless thou drink, no oblivion is thine!

Even if you studied for a hundred years and collected a thousand books, you would not be eligible for the mercy of God the Exalted except through action. [As God says,] 'Man does not receive other than that for which he strives;'[6] 'So let him who hopes for the meeting with his Lord act righteously;'[7] '. . . a reward for what they used to earn;'[8] 'Verily, those who believe and do righteous deeds will have gardens of Paradise, to dwell in forever, whence they will not seek change;'[9]

أَيُّهَا ٱلْوَلَدُ، لَا تَكُنْ مِنَ ٱلْأَعْمَالِ مُفْلِساً وَلَا مِنَ ٱلْأَحْوَالِ خَالِياً، وَتَيَقَّنْ أَنَّ ٱلْعِلْمَ ٱلْمُجَرَّدَ لَا يَأْخُذُ بِٱلْيَدِ. مِثَالُهُ لَوْ كَانَ عَلَى رَجُلٍ فِي بَرِّيَّةٍ عَشَرَةُ أَسْيَافٍ هِنْدِيَّةٍ مَعَ أَسْلِحَةٍ أُخْرَى، وَكَانَ ٱلرَّجُلُ شُجَاعاً وَأَهْلَ حَرْبٍ، فَحَمَلَ عَلَيْهِ أَسَدٌ عَظِيمٌ مَهِيبٌ، فَمَا ظَنُّكَ؟ هَلْ تَدْفَعُ ٱلْأَسْلِحَةُ شَرَّهُ عَنْهُ بِلَا ٱسْتِعْمَالِهَا وَٱلضَّرْبِ بِهَا؟ وَمِنَ ٱلْمَعْلُومِ أَنَّهَا لَا تَدْفَعُ إِلَّا بِٱلتَّحْرِيكِ وَٱلضَّرْبِ.

فَكَذَا لَوْ قَرَأَ رَجُلٌ مِئَةَ أَلْفِ مَسْأَلَةٍ عِلْمِيَّةٍ وَتَعَلَّمَهَا، وَلَمْ يَعْمَلْ بِهَا، لَا تُفِيدُهُ إِلَّا بِٱلْعَمَلِ. وَمِثْلُهُ أَيْضاً لَوْ كَانَ لِرَجُلٍ حَرَارَةٌ وَمَرَضٌ صَفْرَاوِيٌّ يَكُونُ عِلَاجُهُ بِٱلسَّكَنْجَبِينِ وَٱلْكَشْكَابِ، فَلَا يَحْصُلُ ٱلْبُرْءُ إِلَّا بِٱسْتِعْمَالِهِمَا.

گر مي دو هزار رطل همي پيمائي
تا مي نخوري نباشدت شيدائي

وَلَوْ قَرَأْتَ ٱلْعِلْمَ مَائَةَ سَنَةٍ وَجَمَعْتَ أَلْفَ كِتَابٍ، لَا تَكُونُ مُسْتَعِدًّا لِرَحْمَةِ ٱللّٰهِ تَعَالَى إِلَّا بِٱلْعَمَلِ، «وَأَنْ لَيْسَ لِلْإِنْسٰنِ إِلَّا مَا سَعىٰ»، «فَمَنْ كَانَ يَرْجُوا لِقَاءَ رَبِّهِ فَلْيَعْمَلْ عَمَلًا صَالِحًا»، «جَزَآءً بِمَا كَانُوا يَكْسِبُونَ»، «إِنَّ ٱلَّذِينَ آمَنُوا وَعَمِلُوا ٱلصّٰلِحٰتِ كَانَتْ لَهُمْ جَنّٰتُ ٱلْفِرْدَوْسِ نُزُلًا خٰلِدِينَ فِيهَا لَا يَبْغُونَ عَنْهَا حِوَلًا»،

'Descendants have replaced them who neglected prayer and followed passions. They shall come to perdition—except for whoever repents and believes, and acts righteously, for these will enter the Garden and not be harmed at all.'[10]

What say you regarding this Tradition (*ḥadīth*), 'Islam is based on five things: testimony that there is no god but God, and that Muḥammad is the Messenger of God; keeping-up the formal prayer; paying alms; the fast of Ramaḍān; and pilgrimage to the House for whoever is capable of the journey'?[11]

Faith is verbal declaration, consent by the heart, and action in accordance with the [five] pillars—and the evidence of deeds is incalculable, even though the worshipper attains Paradise by the bounty and grace of God the Exalted. Nevertheless [this is] consequent to his being predisposed through obedience to Him and worship of Him, since 'The Mercy of God is near to those who do good.'[12]

If moreover it is said, 'He gets there by faith alone', we reply: Yes, but when will he get there? How many difficult obstacles must he overcome before arriving?[A] And the first of these obstacles is that of faith [itself] and will he be safe from the denial of faith or not, and when he arrives, will he be unsuccessful and destitute? Al-Ḥasan al-Baṣrī said, 'God the Exalted will say to His worshippers on the Day of Resurrection, "O worshippers of Mine, enter the Garden by My mercy and divide it between you according to your deeds."'

أيها الولد

[A]Deeds indicate faith and are part of it: an aspect of what constitutes faith is 'action in accordance with the pillars' (*ʿamal bi 'l-arkān*). Such time as elapses between the incidence of a faith worthy of the name, and death, must be filled with actions consistent with faith.

« فَخَلَفَ مِن بَعْدِهِمْ خَلْفٌ أَضَاعُوا ٱلصَّلَوٰةَ وَٱتَّبَعُوا ٱلشَّهَوٰتِ فَسَوْفَ يَلْقَوْنَ غَيّاً إِلَّا مَنْ تَابَ وَآمَنَ وَعَمِلَ صٰلِحاً فَأُوْلٰئِكَ يَدْخُلُونَ ٱلْجَنَّةَ وَلَا يُظْلَمُونَ شَيْئًا».

وَمَا تَقُولُ فِي هٰذَا ٱلْحَدِيثِ: بُنِيَ ٱلْإِسْلَامُ عَلَى خَمْسٍ: شَهَادَةِ أَنْ لَا إِلٰهَ إِلَّا ٱللّٰهُ وَأَنَّ مُحَمَّداً رَسُولُ ٱللّٰهِ، وَإِقَامِ ٱلصَّلَاةِ، وَإِيتَاءِ ٱلزَّكَاةِ، وَصَوْمِ رَمَضَانَ، وَحَجِّ ٱلْبَيْتِ لِمَنْ ٱسْتَطَاعَ إِلَيْهِ سَبِيلاً.

وَٱلْإِيمَانُ قَوْلٌ بِٱللِّسَانِ وَتَصْدِيقٌ بِٱلْجَنَانِ وَعَمَلٌ بِٱلْأَرْكَانِ. وَدَلِيلُ ٱلْأَعْمَالِ أَكْثَرُ مِنْ أَنْ يُحْصَى، وَإِنْ كَانَ ٱلْعَبْدُ يَبْلُغُ ٱلْجَنَّةَ بِفَضْلِ ٱللّٰهِ تَعَالَى وَكَرَمِهِ، لٰكِنْ بَعْدَ أَنْ يَسْتَعِدَّ بِطَاعَتِهِ وَعِبَادَتِهِ، لِأَنَّ «رَحْمَتَ ٱللّٰهِ قَرِيبٌ مِنَ ٱلْمُحْسِنِينَ».

وَلَوْ قِيلَ أَيْضاً: يَبْلُغُ بِمُجَرَّدِ ٱلْإِيمَانِ، قُلْنَا: نَعَمْ، لٰكِنْ مَتَى يَبْلُغُ؟ وَكَمْ مِنْ عَقَبَةٍ كَؤُودٍ يَقْطَعُهَا إِلَى أَنْ يَصِلَ؟ فَأَوَّلُ تِلْكَ ٱلْعَقَبَاتِ عَقَبَةُ ٱلْإِيمَانِ، وَأَنَّهُ هَلْ يَسْلَمُ مِنْ سَلْبِ ٱلْإِيمَانِ أَمْ لَا؟ وَإِذَا وَصَلَ هَلْ يَكُونُ خَائِباً مُفْلِساً؟ وَقَالَ ٱلْحَسَنُ ٱلْبَصْرِيُّ: يَقُولُ ٱللّٰهُ تَعَالَى لِعِبَادِهِ يَوْمَ ٱلْقِيَامَةِ: ٱدْخُلُوا، يَا عِبَادِي، ٱلْجَنَّةَ بِرَحْمَتِي وَٱقْتَسِمُوهَا بِأَعْمَالِكُمْ.

أيها الولد

O disciple, insofar as you do not act, you will not find recompense. It is related that a man from the tribe of Israel worshipped God the Exalted for seventy years. Thus God the Exalted wished to show him to the angels, so He sent an angel to him to inform him that in spite of this worship, entering the Garden was not fitting for him. When he heard this the worshipper replied, 'We are created for worship and it is incumbent on us to worship Him!' When the angel went back he said, 'My God, you know best what he said.' God the Exalted replied, 'Since he did not turn away from worshipping Us, We will not turn away from him with [Our] grace! Witness O angels of Mine, that I have forgiven Him.'[A]

God's Messenger (God bless him and give him peace) said, 'Call yourselves to account before you are called to account, and weigh up your deeds before they are weighed for you.'[13] And ʿAlī (may God be pleased with him) said, 'Whoso believes that he will attain his goal without effort is a wishful thinker. And whoso believes he will reach his goal by the expending of effort is presumptuous.' Al-Ḥasan (may God the Exalted be merciful to him) said, 'Seeking the Garden without action is a sin,' and he said, 'An indication of the true state of affairs is to give up paying attention to action, not to give up action.' And the Messenger of God (God bless him and give him peace) said, 'The astute man is one who passes judgement on himself and works for what is after death, and the fool is one who pursues vain pleasures and counts on God the Exalted to realize his wishes.'[14]

أيها الولد

[A] God's forgiveness in this case—evidently that of a fundamentally saintly soul—presumably pertains to his inadvertent and minor sins.

أَيُّهَا ٱلْوَلَدُ، مَا لَمْ تَعْمَلْ لَمْ تَجِدِ ٱلْأَجْرَ. حُكِيَ أَنَّ رَجُلاً مِنْ بَنِي إِسْرَائِيلَ عَبَدَ ٱللهَ تَعَالَى سَبْعِينَ سَنَةً. فَأَرَادَ ٱللهُ تَعَالَى أَنْ يَجْلُوَهُ عَلَى ٱلْمَلَائِكَةِ، فَأَرْسَلَ ٱللهُ إِلَيْهِ مَلَكاً يُخْبِرُهُ أَنَّهُ مَعَ تِلْكَ ٱلْعِبَادَةِ لَا يَلِيقُ بِهِ دُخُولُ ٱلْجَنَّةِ. فَلَمَّا بَلَغَهُ قَالَ ٱلْعَابِدُ: نَحْنُ خُلِقْنَا لِلْعِبَادَةِ فَيَنْبَغِي لَنَا أَنْ نَعْبُدَهُ. فَلَمَّا رَجَعَ ٱلْمَلَكُ قَالَ: إِلٰهِي أَنْتَ أَعْلَمُ بِمَا قَالَ. فَقَالَ ٱللهُ تَعَالَى: إِذَا هُوَ لَمْ يُعْرِضْ عَنْ عِبَادَتِنَا فَنَحْنُ مَعَ ٱلْكَرَمِ لَا نُعْرِضُ عَنْهُ. إِشْهَدُوا يَا مَلَائِكَتِي أَنِّي قَدْ غَفَرْتُ لَهُ.

وَقَالَ رَسُولُ ٱللهِ، صَلَّى ٱللهُ عَلَيْهِ وَسَلَّمَ: حَاسِبُوا أَنْفُسَكُمْ قَبْلَ أَنْ تُحَاسَبُوا، وَزِنُوا أَعْمَالَكُمْ قَبْلَ أَنْ تُوزَنَ عَلَيْكُمْ. وَقَالَ عَلِيٌّ، رَضِيَ ٱللهُ عَنْهُ: مَنْ ظَنَّ أَنَّهُ بِدُونِ ٱلْجَهْدِ يَصِلُ فَهُوَ مُتَمَنٍّ. وَمَنْ ظَنَّ أَنَّهُ بِبَذْلِ ٱلْجَهْدِ يَصِلُ فَهُوَ مُسْتَغْنٍ. وَقَالَ ٱلْحَسَنُ، رَحِمَهُ ٱللهُ تَعَالَى: طَلَبُ ٱلْجَنَّةِ بِلَا عَمَلٍ ذَنْبٌ مِنَ ٱلذُّنُوبِ. وَقَالَ: عَلَامَةُ ٱلْحَقِيقَةِ تَرْكُ مُلَاحَظَةِ ٱلْعَمَلِ لَا تَرْكُ ٱلْعَمَلِ. وَقَالَ رَسُولُ ٱللهِ، صَلَّى ٱللهُ عَلَيْهِ وَسَلَّمَ: ٱلْكَيِّسُ مَنْ دَانَ نَفْسَهُ وَعَمِلَ لِمَا بَعْدَ ٱلْمَوْتِ، وَٱلْأَحْمَقُ مَنِ ٱتَّبَعَ هَوَاهُ وَتَمَنَّى عَلَى ٱللهِ تَعَالَى ٱلْأَمَانِيَّ.

O disciple, how many nights have you spent rehearsing your learning, reading books, and depriving yourself of sleep? I do not know what the motive was in this—if it was winning the goods of the world, the allure of its vanities, getting its honours, and vainglory to the debit of your associates and peers, woe to you and woe again! But if your objective in it was the revival of the Prophet's Law (God bless him and give him peace), the cultivation of your character and breaking the 'soul that inciteth to evil,'[15] blessing upon you and blessing again! He has told the truth who spoke the verse:

> Sleeplessness of the eye but for Thy sake is vain,
> Their crying but for Thy loss inane.

أيها الولد

O disciple: 'Live as long as you want, but you must die; love whatever you want, but you will become separated from it; and do what you want, but you will be repaid for it!'[16]

O disciple, what result have you had from studying the science of scholastic theology (*kalām*), rhetoric, medicine, collections of poems, astronomy, metrics, grammar and inflections, other than wasting your life in opposition to the Lord

أَيُّهَا ٱلْوَلَدُ، كَمْ مِنْ لَيَالٍ أَحْيَيْتَهَا بِتَكْرَارِ ٱلْعِلْمِ وَمُطَالَعَةِ ٱلْكُتُبِ وَحَرَّمْتَ عَلَى نَفْسِكَ ٱلنَّوْمَ؟ لَا أَعْلَمُ مَا كَانَ ٱلْبَاعِثُ فِيهِ. إِنْ كَانَ نَيْلَ عَرَضِ ٱلدُّنْيَا وَجَذْبَ حُطَامِهَا وَتَحْصِيلَ مَنَاصِبِهَا وَٱلْمُبَاهَاةَ عَلَى ٱلْأَقْرَانِ وَٱلْأَمْثَالِ، فَوَيْلٌ لَكَ ثُمَّ وَيْلٌ لَكَ. وَإِنْ كَانَ قَصْدُكَ فِيهِ إِحْيَاءَ شَرِيعَةِ ٱلنَّبِيِّ، صَلَّى ٱللهُ عَلَيْهِ وَسَلَّمَ، وَتَهْذِيبَ أَخْلَاقِكَ وَكَسْرَ ٱلنَّفْسِ ٱلْأَمَّارَةِ بِٱلسُّوءِ، فَطُوبَى لَكَ ثُمَّ طُوبَى لَكَ. وَلَقَدْ صَدَقَ مَنْ قَالَ شِعْراً:

سَهَرُ ٱلْعُيُونِ لِغَيْرِ وَجْهِكَ ضَائِعٌ
وَبُكَاؤُهُنَّ لِغَيْرِ فَقْدِكَ بَاطِلٌ

أيها الولد

أَيُّهَا ٱلْوَلَدُ: عِشْ مَا شِئْتَ فَإِنَّكَ مَيِّتٌ، وَأَحْبِبْ مَا شِئْتَ فَإِنَّكَ مُفَارِقُهُ، وَٱعْمَلْ مَا شِئْتَ فَإِنَّكَ مَجْزِيٌّ بِهِ.

أَيُّهَا ٱلْوَلَدُ، أَيُّ شَيْءٍ حَاصِلٌ لَكَ مِنْ تَحْصِيلِ عِلْمِ ٱلْكَلَامِ وَٱلْخِلَافِ وَٱلطِّبِّ وَٱلدَّوَاوِينِ وَٱلْأَشْعَارِ وَٱلنُّجُومِ وَٱلْعَرُوضِ وَٱلنَّحْوِ وَٱلتَّصْرِيفِ غَيْرُ تَضْيِيعِ ٱلْعُمُرِ بِخِلَافِ ذِي ٱلْجَلَالِ.

of Majesty? I have seen in the Gospel of Jesus (upon him be blessings and peace), 'From the moment the dead man is put on the bier till he is put at the graveside, God in His Majesty will ask him forty questions. The first of them is, "Worshipper of Mine, for years you purified yourself in view of men and not for one hour did you purify yourself in view of Me."[17] And every day He looks into your heart He says, "What is this you are doing for others than Myself, when it is My goodness with which you are surrounded? But as for you, you are deaf and heedless!"'

أيها الولد

O disciple, knowledge without action is madness and action without knowledge is void. Know that the knowledge which does not remove you from sins today and does not convert you to obedience, will not remove you tomorrow from hellfire. If you do not act according to your knowledge today, and you do not make amends for days gone-by, you will say tomorrow on the Day of Resurrection, 'Send us back and we will act virtuously!'[18] And it will be replied, 'Fool! You have just come from there!'

أيها الولد

O disciple, get zeal in respect of the spirit, subdual in respect of the ego and mortification in respect of the body, for your destination is the grave, and the people of the graves expect you at any moment to meet up with them. Beware, beware lest you meet up with them without provision!

إِنِّي رَأَيْتُ فِي إِنْجِيلِ عِيسَى، عَلَيْهِ ٱلصَّلَاةُ وَٱلسَّلَامُ: مِنْ سَاعَةِ أَنْ يُوضَعَ ٱلْمَيِّتُ عَلَى ٱلْجِنَازَةِ إِلَى أَنْ يُوضَعَ عَلَى شَفِيرِ ٱلْقَبْرِ يَسْأَلُ ٱللّٰهُ بِعَظَمَتِهِ مِنْهُ أَرْبَعِينَ سُؤَالاً. أَوَّلُهَا يَقُولُ: عَبْدِي طَهَّرْتَ مَنْظَرَ ٱلْخَلْقِ سِنِينَ وَمَا طَهَّرْتَ مَنْظَرِي سَاعَةً. وَكُلَّ يَوْمٍ يَنْظُرُ فِي قَلْبِكَ يَقُولُ: مَا تَصْنَعُ لِغَيْرِي وَأَنْتَ مَحْفُوفٌ بِخَيْرِي. أَمَّا أَنْتَ فَأَصَمٌّ لَا تَسْمَعُ.

أيها الولد

أَيُّهَا ٱلْوَلَدُ، اَلْعِلْمُ بِلَا عَمَلٍ جُنُونٌ، وَٱلْعَمَلُ بِغَيْرِ عِلْمٍ لَا يَكُونُ. وَٱعْلَمْ أَنَّ ٱلْعِلْمَ ٱلَّذِي لَا يُبْعِدُكَ ٱلْيَوْمَ عَنِ ٱلْمَعَاصِي وَلَا يَحْمِلُكَ عَلَى ٱلطَّاعَةِ لَنْ يُبْعِدَكَ غَداً عَنْ نَارِ جَهَنَّمَ. وَإِذَا لَمْ تَعْمَلْ بِعِلْمِكَ ٱلْيَوْمَ وَلَمْ تَدَارَكِ ٱلْأَيَّامَ ٱلْمَاضِيَةَ تَقُولُ غَداً يَوْمَ ٱلْقِيَامَةِ: «فَأَرْجِعْنَا نَعْمَلْ صٰلِحاً» فَيُقَالُ: يَا أَحْمَقُ أَنْتَ مِنْ هُنَاكَ تَجِيءُ.

أيها الولد

أَيُّهَا ٱلْوَلَدُ، إِجْعَلِ ٱلْهِمَّةَ فِي ٱلرُّوحِ وَٱلْهَزِيمَةَ فِي ٱلنَّفْسِ وَٱلْمَوْتَ فِي ٱلْبَدَنِ لِأَنَّ مَنْزِلَكَ ٱلْقَبْرُ وَأَهْلُ ٱلْمَقَابِرِ يَنْتَظِرُونَكَ فِي كُلِّ لَحْظَةٍ مَتَى تَصِلُ إِلَيْهِمْ. إِيَّاكَ إِيَّاكَ أَنْ تَصِلَ إِلَيْهِمْ بِلَا زَادٍ.

Abū Bakr al-Ṣiddīq (may God be pleased with him) said, 'These bodies are a cage for birds or a stable for beasts.' Think about yourself—which of them are you? If you are one of the heavenly birds, when you hear the sound of the drumbeat of 'Return to your Lord'[19] you will fly upwards till you roost on the highest towers in the Gardens, as God's Messenger (God bless him and give him peace) said, 'The throne of the Infinitely Good trembled from the death of Saʿd ibn Muʿādh.'[A][20] And God forbid if you are one of the beasts! As God the Exalted said, 'They are as cattle, nay, they are more astray.'[21] Let yourself not feel safe from being removed from the corner of your home to the chasm of hellfire!

It is related that al-Ḥasan al-Baṣrī (may God the Exalted have mercy on him) was given a drink of cold water. So he took the cup and he fainted, and it dropped from his hand. When he came to, it was said, 'What happened, Abū Saʿīd ?' He replied, 'I recalled the longing of the people of hellfire, when they will say to the people of the Garden, "Pour down water upon us—or whatever God has bestowed upon you."'[22]

أيها الولد

O disciple, if mere knowledge were enough for you and you did not need deeds besides it, His call 'Is there any suppliant? Is there anyone seeking forgiveness? Is there anyone repentant?'[B] would be superfluous, and without purpose. It is related that a group of the Companions (God's good-pleasure

[A] Ghazālī's point in citing this somewhat unexpected Tradition is that it indicates the degree of proximity to God attainable by the virtuous. There is implicit the interpretation that the 'highest towers' are close by (or even the same as) God's throne, such that Saʿd's 'roosting' makes it tremble or shake.

[B] The words are from a Tradition according to which, God, during the last third of the night, descends to the lowest heaven and asks these questions of any who are awake and praying. Bukhārī, *Tahajjud*, 14; *Tawḥīd*, 35, *Daʿawāt*, 12; Muslim, *Musāfirīn*, 168–170; Abū Dāūd, *Sunna*, 19; Tirmidhī, *Ṣalā*, 168; Mālik, *Qur'ān*, 30; Ibn Ḥanbal, 4.16.

قَالَ أَبُو بَكْرٍ ٱلصِّدِّيقُ، رَضِيَ ٱللّٰهُ عَنْهُ: هَذِهِ ٱلْأَجْسَادُ قَفَصُ ٱلطُّيُورِ أَوْ إِصْطَبْلُ ٱلدَّوَابِّ. فَتَفَكَّرْ فِي نَفْسِكَ: مِنْ أَيِّهِمَا أَنْتَ؟ إِنْ كُنْتَ مِنَ ٱلطُّيُورِ ٱلْعُلْوِيَّةِ فَحِينَ تَسْمَعُ طَنِينَ طَبْلِ «إِرْجِعِي إِلَى رَبِّكِ» تَطِيرُ صَاعِداً إِلَى أَنْ تَقْعُدَ فِي أَعَالِي بُرُوجِ ٱلْجِنَانِ، كَمَا قَالَ رَسُولُ ٱللّٰهِ، صَلَّى ٱللّٰهُ عَلَيْهِ وَسَلَّمَ: اَهْتَزَّ عَرْشُ ٱلرَّحْمٰنِ مِنْ مَوْتِ سَعْدِ بْنِ مُعَاذٍ. وَٱلْعِيَاذُ بِٱللّٰهِ إِنْ كُنْتَ مِنَ ٱلدَّوَابِّ، كَمَا قَالَ ٱللّٰهُ تَعَالَى: «أُولٰئِكَ كَٱلْأَنْعَمِ بَلْ هُمْ أَضَلُّ.» فَلَا تَأْمَنِ ٱنْتِقَالَكَ مِنْ زَاوِيَةِ ٱلدَّارِ إِلَى هَاوِيَةِ ٱلنَّارِ.

وَرُوِيَ أَنَّ ٱلْحَسَنَ ٱلْبَصْرِيَّ، رَحِمَهُ ٱللّٰهُ تَعَالَى، أُعْطِيَ شَرْبَةَ مَاءٍ بَارِدٍ، فَأَخَذَ ٱلْقَدَحَ وَغُشِيَ عَلَيْهِ وَسَقَطَ مِنْ يَدِهِ. فَلَمَّا أَفَاقَ قِيلَ: مَا لَكَ يَا أَبَا سَعِيدٍ؟ قَالَ: ذَكَرْتُ أُمْنِيَّةَ أَهْلِ ٱلنَّارِ حِينَ يَقُولُونَ لِأَهْلِ ٱلْجَنَّةِ: أَنْ أَفِيضُوا عَلَيْنَا مِنَ ٱلْمَاءِ أَوْ مِمَّا رَزَقَكُمُ ٱللّٰهُ.

أيها الولد

أَيُّهَا ٱلْوَلَدُ، لَوْ كَانَ ٱلْعِلْمُ ٱلْمُجَرَّدُ كَافِياً لَكَ وَلَا تَحْتَاجُ إِلَى عَمَلٍ سِوَاهُ لَكَانَ نِدَاءُ: هَلْ مِنْ سَائِلٍ؟ هَلْ مِنْ مُسْتَغْفِرٍ؟ هَلْ مِنْ تَائِبٍ؟ ضَائِعاً بِلَا فَائِدَةٍ. وَرُوِيَ أَنَّ جَمَاعَةً مِنَ ٱلصَّحَابَةِ، رِضْوَانُ

be upon them all) mentioned ʿAbd Allāh the son of ʿUmar (may God be pleased with both) in the presence of the Messenger of God (God bless him and give him peace), and he said, 'What an excellent man he is. If only he would pray at night!'[23] And he said (upon him be blessings and peace) to a man from among his Companions, 'O so and so, do not sleep much at night, for a large quantity of sleep at night will leave its owner a poor man on Resurrection Day.'[24]

أيها الولد

O disciple, 'And part of the night keep vigil as a work of supererogation for you'[25] is a command, 'And before daybreak they (i.e. the God-conscious) seek forgiveness'[26] is a commendation, 'And those seeking forgiveness before daybreak'[27] is a reminder.

He (upon him be peace) said, 'Three voices are loved by God the Exalted—the cock's crow, the voice of him who recites the Qur'ān, and the voice of those seeking forgiveness before daybreak.'[28] Sufyān al-Thawrī (the mercy of God the Exalted be upon him) said, 'God, Blessed and Exalted, created a wind, blowing before daybreak, carrying invocations and prayers for forgiveness to the Almighty King.' He also said, 'At the start of the night a crier calls from beneath the Throne, "Let the worshippers get up!" So they get up and they pray as God wills. Then a crier calls at midnight, "Let those who stand at length in prayer get up!" So they get up and they pray until before daybreak. And when it is before daybreak a crier calls, "Let those seeking forgiveness get up!" So they get up and seek forgiveness. And when the dawn breaks a crier calls, "Let the heedless get up!" So they get out of their beds like the dead risen from their graves.'

أيها الولد

ٱللهِ عَلَيْهِمْ أَجْمَعِينَ، ذَكَرُوا عَبْدَ ٱللهِ بْنَ عُمَرَ، رَضِيَ ٱللهُ عَنْهُمَا، عِنْدَ رَسُولِ ٱللهِ، صَلَّى ٱللهُ عَلَيْهِ وَسَلَّمَ، فَقَالَ: نِعْمَ ٱلرَّجُلُ هُوَ لَوْ كَانَ يُصَلِّي بِٱللَّيْلِ. وَقَالَ عَلَيْهِ ٱلصَّلَاةُ وَٱلسَّلَامُ لِرَجُلٍ مِنْ أَصْحَابِهِ: يَا فُلَانُ، لَا تُكْثِرِ ٱلنَّوْمَ بِٱللَّيْلِ فَإِنَّ كَثْرَةَ ٱلنَّوْمِ بِٱللَّيْلِ تَدَعُ صَاحِبَهُ فَقِيراً يَوْمَ ٱلْقِيَامَةِ.

أيها الولد

أَيُّهَا ٱلْوَلَدُ، «وَمِنَ ٱلَّيْلِ فَتَهَجَّدْ بِهِ نَافِلَةً لَكَ» أَمْرٌ، «وَبِٱلْأَسْحَارِ هُمْ يَسْتَغْفِرُونَ» شُكْرٌ، «وَٱلْمُسْتَغْفِرِينَ بِٱلْأَسْحَارِ» ذِكْرٌ.

قَالَ عَلَيْهِ ٱلسَّلَامُ: ثَلَاثَةُ أَصْوَاتٍ يُحِبُّهَا ٱللهُ تَعَالَى: صَوْتُ ٱلدِّيكِ، وَصَوْتُ ٱلَّذِي يَقْرَأُ ٱلْقُرْآنَ، وَصَوْتُ ٱلْمُسْتَغْفِرِينَ بِٱلْأَسْحَارِ. قَالَ سُفْيَانُ ٱلثَّوْرِيُّ، رَحْمَةُ ٱللهِ تَعَالَى عَلَيْهِ: إِنَّ ٱللهَ تَبَارَكَ وَتَعَالَى خَلَقَ رِيحاً تَهُبُّ بِٱلْأَسْحَارِ تَحْمِلُ ٱلْأَذْكَارَ وَٱلإِسْتِغْفَارَ إِلَى ٱلْمَلِكِ ٱلْجَبَّارِ. وَقَالَ أَيْضاً: إِذَا كَانَ أَوَّلُ ٱللَّيْلِ، يُنَادِي مُنَادٍ مِنْ تَحْتِ ٱلْعَرْشِ: أَلَا لِيَقُمِ ٱلْعَابِدُونَ. فَيَقُومُونَ وَيُصَلُّونَ مَا شَاءَ ٱللهُ. ثُمَّ يُنَادِي مُنَادٍ فِي شَطْرِ ٱللَّيْلِ: أَلَا لِيَقُمِ ٱلْقَانِتُونَ. فَيَقُومُونَ وَيُصَلُّونَ إِلَى ٱلسَّحَرِ. فَإِذَا كَانَ ٱلسَّحَرُ نَادَى مُنَادٍ: أَلَا لِيَقُمِ ٱلْمُسْتَغْفِرُونَ. فَيَقُومُونَ وَيَسْتَغْفِرُونَ. فَإِذَا طَلَعَ ٱلْفَجْرُ نَادَى مُنَادٍ: أَلَا لِيَقُمِ ٱلْغَافِلُونَ. فَيَقُومُونَ مِنْ فُرُشِهِمْ كَٱلْمَوْتَى نُشِرُوا مِنْ قُبُورِهِمْ.

أيها الولد

O disciple, in the advice Luqmān the Wise gave his son it is related that he said, 'My son, do not ever let the cock be more canny than yourself. He calls out before daybreak while you are sleeping.' He has done well who spoke the verse,

A dove moaned frailly in the dark one night
On a branch, while I was sleeping.
I have lied, by God's House! Were I a lover,
Then doves wouldn't beat me in weeping.
I claim I am mad with love, fervent with longing
For my Lord, yet I do not weep and such animals
are weeping.

أيها الولد

O disciple, the essence of knowledge is to know what obedience and worship are. Know that obedience and worship are conformity to the Lawgiver as regards commands and prohibitions, in both word and deed. That is, all that you say and do, or do not do, should be following the paradigm of the Law, such that were you to fast on the day of the ʿĪd feast and the Days of the Tashrīq[A] you would be a rebel. Or if you prayed in a garment unlawfully acquired, though there is the appearance of worship, you sin.

أيها الولد

[A]The Days of the Tashrīq are the three days following the festival of ʿĪd al-Aḍḥā at the end of the Greater Pilgrimage (*Ḥajj*).

أَيُّهَا ٱلْوَلَدُ، رُوِيَ فِي وَصَايَا لُقْمَانَ ٱلْحَكِيمِ لِٱبْنِهِ أَنَّـهُ قَالَ: يَا بُنَيَّ، لَا يَكُونَنَّ ٱلدِّيكُ أَكْيَسَ مِنْكَ. يُنَادِي بِٱلْأَسْحَارِ وَأَنْتَ نَائِمٌ. وَلَقَدْ أَحْسَنَ مَنْ قَالَ شِعْراً:

لَقَدْ هَتَفَتْ فِي جُنْحِ لَيْلٍ حَمَامَةٌ
عَلَى فَنَنٍ وَهْناً وَإِنِّي لَنَائِمُ
كَذَبْتُ، وَبَيْتِ ٱللهِ، لَوْ كُنْتُ عَاشِقاً
لَمَا سَبَقَتْنِي بِٱلْبُكَاءِ ٱلْحَمَائِمُ
وَأَزْعُمُ أَنِّي هَائِـمٌ ذُو صَبَابَةٍ
لِرَبِّي، فَلَا أَبْكِي وَتَبْكِي ٱلْبَهَائِـمُ

أيها الولد

أَيُّهَا ٱلْوَلَدُ، خُلَاصَةُ ٱلْعِلْمِ أَنْ تَعْلَمَ ٱلطَّاعَةَ وَٱلْعِبَادَةَ مَا هِيَ. إِعْلَمْ أَنَّ ٱلطَّاعَةَ وَٱلْعِبَادَةَ مُتَابَعَةُ ٱلشَّارِعِ فِي ٱلْأَوَامِرِ وَٱلنَّوَاهِي بِٱلْقَوْلِ وَٱلْفِعْلِ. يَعْنِي: كُلُّ مَا تَقُولُ وَتَفْعَلُ وَتَتْرُكُ يَكُونُ بِٱقْتِدَاءِ ٱلشَّرْعِ، كَمَا لَوْ صُمْتَ يَوْمَ ٱلْعِيدِ وَأَيَّامَ ٱلتَّشْرِيقِ تَكُونُ عَاصِياً، أَوْ صَلَّيْتَ فِي ثَوْبٍ مَغْصُوبٍ، وَإِنْ كَانَتْ صُورَةَ عِبَادَةٍ، تَأْثَمُ.

أيها الولد

O disciple, it is desirable for you that your speech and action be in accord with the Law, since knowledge and action which are not modelled on the Law are error. And you must not be deceived by the ecstatic expressions and outbursts of the Sufis, since travel on this path should be by way of self-exertion, severing the ego's appetite and killing its passions with the sword of discipline, and not by way of outbursts and useless statements.

Know that the unrestrained tongue, and the heart that is rusted over and full of negligence and greed, are a sign of misfortune, and if you do not kill the ego with sincere exertion your heart will not be animated by the lights of gnosis.

Know that the answers to some of the things about which you asked me are not brought about through writing and discussion. If you attain to that state you will know what they are, and if not—knowing them is an impossibility, in that they pertain to direct experience. The description of anything to do with direct experience is not furnished through discussion, as the sweetness of what is sweet and the bitterness of what is bitter is not known except by taste. Thus it was related that an impotent man wrote to a friend of his to tell him what the pleasure of sex was like. So he wrote back to him in reply, 'O so and so, I thought you were just impotent! Now I know that you are impotent *and* stupid, since this pleasure is to do with direct experience—if you attain it you know it—otherwise the description of it is not furnished through talking and writing!'

أيها الولد

أَيُّهَا ٱلْوَلَدُ، يَنْبَغِي لَكَ أَنْ يَكُونَ قَوْلُكَ وَفِعْلُكَ مُوافِقاً لِلشَّرْعِ، إِذِ ٱلْعِلْمُ وَٱلْعَمَلُ بِلَا ٱقْتِدَاءٍ لِلشَّرْعِ ضَلَالَةٌ، وَيَنْبَغِي لَكَ أَلَّا تَغْتَرَّ بِٱلشَّطْحِ وَطَامَّاتِ ٱلصُّوفِيَّةِ، لِأَنَّ سُلُوكَ هٰذَا ٱلطَّرِيقِ يَكُونَ بِٱلْمُجَاهَدَةِ وَقَطْعِ شَهْوَةِ ٱلنَّفْسِ وَقَتْلِ هَوَاهَا بِسَيْفِ ٱلرِّيَاضَةِ، لَا بِٱلطَّامَّاتِ وَٱلتُّرَّهَاتِ.

وَٱعْلَمْ أَنَّ ٱللِّسَانَ ٱلْمُطْلَقَ وَٱلْقَلْبَ ٱلْمُطْبَقَ ٱلْمَمْلُوءَ بِٱلْغَفْلَةِ وَٱلشَّهْوَةِ عَلَامَةُ ٱلشَّقَاوَةِ. فَإِذَا لَمْ تَقْتُلِ ٱلنَّفْسَ بِصِدْقِ ٱلْمُجَاهَدَةِ فَلَنْ يَحْيَا قَلْبُكَ بِأَنْوَارِ ٱلْمَعْرِفَةِ.

وَٱعْلَمْ أَنَّ بَعْضَ مَسَائِلِكَ ٱلَّتِي سَأَلْتَنِي عَنْهَا لَا يَسْتَقِيمُ جَوَابُهَا بِٱلْكِتَابَةِ وَٱلْقَوْلِ. إِنْ تَبْلُغْ تِلْكَ ٱلْحَالَةَ تَعْرِفْ مَا هِيَ، وَإِلَّا فَعِلْمُهَا مِنَ ٱلْمُسْتَحِيلَاتِ لِأَنَّهَا ذَوْقِيَّةٌ، وَكُلُّ مَا يَكُونُ ذَوْقِيّاً لَا يَسْتَقِيمُ وَصْفُهُ بِٱلْقَوْلِ كَحَلَاوَةِ ٱلْحُلْوِ وَمَرَارَةِ ٱلْمُرِّ لَا تُعْرَفُ إِلَّا بِٱلذَّوْقِ. كَمَا حُكِيَ أَنَّ عِنِّيناً كَتَبَ إِلَى صَاحِبٍ لَهُ أَنْ عَرِّفْنِي لَذَّةَ ٱلْمُجَامَعَةِ كَيْفَ تَكُونُ. فَكَتَبَ لَهُ فِي جَوَابِهِ: يَا فُلَانُ إِنِّي كُنْتُ حَسِبْتُكَ عِنِّيناً فَقَطْ، وَٱلْآنَ عَرَفْتُ أَنَّكَ عِنِّينٌ وَأَحْمَقُ. لِأَنَّ هٰذِهِ ٱللَّذَّةَ ذَوْقِيَّةٌ إِنْ تَصِلْ إِلَيْهَا تَعْرِفْ، وَإِلَّا لَا يَسْتَقِيمُ وَصْفُهَا بِٱلْقَوْلِ وَٱلْكِتَابَةِ.

O disciple, some of your questions are of this sort, and as for those capable of being answered, we have mentioned them in the *Revival of the Sciences* and other works. We mention here excerpts from it while referring you to it. We say: the spiritual traveller needs four things. The first thing is an authentic creed which contains no innovation. The second is true contrition after which there is no going back to re-offending. The third is reconciliation with enemies, so that none of them retains a claim against you. The fourth is obtaining enough knowledge of the Sharīʿa for the commands of God the Exalted to be executed, then whatever of the other sciences through which there is salvation.

It is related that Shiblī (may God be merciful to him) served four hundred masters and he said, 'I studied four thousand Traditions, then I chose a single Tradition out of them, and acted in accordance with it, giving up the rest, for I meditated on it and I found my deliverance and salvation in it, the knowledge of the ancients and the moderns being all included in it I contented myself with it, and it is that the Messenger of God (may God bless him and give him peace) said to one of his Companions, "Work for your terrestrial life in proportion to your stay in it, and work for your afterlife in proportion to your eternity in it! Work for God in proportion to your need for Him, and work for the Fire in proportion to your ability to endure it!"'[29]

أَيُّهَا ٱلْوَلَدُ، بَعْضُ مَسَائِلِكَ مِنْ هٰذَا ٱلْقَبِيلِ، وَأَمَّا ٱلْبَعْضُ ٱلَّذِي يَسْتَقِيمُ لَهُ ٱلْجَوَابُ فَقَدْ ذَكَرْنَاهُ فِي إِحْيَاءِ ٱلْعُلُومِ وَغَيْرِهِ، وَنَذْكُرُ هَاهُنَا نُبَذاً مِنْهُ وَنُشِيرُ إِلَيْهِ فَنَقُولُ: قَدْ وَجَبَ عَلَى ٱلسَّالِكِ أَرْبَعَةُ أُمُورٍ: اَلْأَمْرُ ٱلْأَوَّلُ ٱعْتِقَادٌ صَحِيحٌ لَا يَكُونُ فِيهِ بِدْعَةٌ. وَٱلثَّانِي تَوْبَةٌ نَصُوحٌ لَا يُرْجَعُ بَعْدَهَا إِلَى ٱلزَّلَّةِ. وَٱلثَّالِثُ إِسْتِرْضَاءُ ٱلْخُصُومِ حَتَّى لَا يَبْقَى لِأَحَدٍ عَلَيْكَ حَقٌّ. وَٱلرَّابِعُ تَحْصِيلُ عِلْمِ ٱلشَّرِيعَةِ قَدْرَ مَا تُؤَدَّى بِهِ أَوَامِرُ ٱللهِ تَعَالَى، ثُمَّ مِنَ ٱلْعُلُومِ ٱلْأُخْرَى مَا تَكُونُ بِهِ ٱلنَّجَاةُ.

حُكِيَ أَنَّ ٱلشِّبْلِيَّ، رَحِمَهُ ٱللهُ، خَدَمَ أَرْبَعَمَائَةَ أُسْتَاذٍ؛ وَقَالَ: قَرَأْتُ أَرْبَعَةَ آلَافِ حَدِيثٍ، ثُمَّ ٱخْتَرْتُ مِنْهَا حَدِيثًا وَاحِدًا وَعَمِلْتُ بِهِ وَخَلَّيْتُ مَا سِوَاهُ لِأَنِّي تَأَمَّلْتُهُ فَوَجَدْتُ خَلَاصِي وَنَجَاتِي فِيهِ، وَكَانَ عِلْمُ ٱلْأَوَّلِينَ وَٱلْآخِرِينَ كُلُّهُ مُنْدَرِجًا فِيهِ فَٱكْتَفَيْتُ بِهِ، وَذٰلِكَ أَنَّ رَسُولَ ٱللهِ، صَلَّى ٱللهُ عَلَيْهِ وَسَلَّمَ، قَالَ لِبَعْضِ أَصْحَابِهِ: إِعْمَلْ لِدُنْيَاكَ بِقَدْرِ مُقَامِكَ فِيهَا، وَٱعْمَلْ لِآخِرَتِكَ بِقَدْرِ بَقَائِكَ فِيهَا، وَٱعْمَلْ لِلّٰهِ بِقَدْرِ حَاجَتِكَ إِلَيْهِ، وَٱعْمَلْ لِلنَّارِ بِقَدْرِ صَبْرِكَ عَلَيْهَا.

أيها الولد

O disciple, if you have knowledge of this Tradition, there is no need for much learning.

Meditate on some other quotations: Ḥātim al-Aṣamm was one of the companions of Shaqīq al-Balkhī (the mercy of God the Exalted be upon them both), and one day he asked him and said, 'You have kept company with me for thirty years. What have you got out of them?' He replied, 'I got eight useful lessons by way of knowledge and they are enough of it for me, for I hope for my deliverance and salvation because of them.' So Shaqīq said, 'What are they?' Ḥātim al-Aṣamm replied:

'[The first useful lesson is that] I observed mankind, and saw that everyone had an object of love and of infatuation which he loved and with which he was infatuated. Some of what was loved accompanied him up to the sickness of death and some [even] up to the graveside. Then all went back and left him solitary and alone, and not one of them entered his grave with him. So I pondered and I said: the best of what one loves is what will enter one's grave and be a friend to one in it. And I found [it to be] nothing but good deeds! So I took them as the object of my love, to be a light for me in my grave, to be a friend to me in it and not leave me all alone.

'[The second useful lesson is that] I saw mankind being guided by their pleasures and hurrying to what their egos desired, so I meditated on His saying (the Exalted), "But as for

أَيُّهَا ٱلْوَلَدُ، إِذَا عَلِمْتَ هٰذَا ٱلْحَدِيثَ، لَا حَاجَةَ إِلَى ٱلْعِلْمِ ٱلْكَثِيرِ.

وَتَأَمَّلْ فِي حِكَايَاتٍ أُخْرَى، وَذَلِكَ أَنَّ حَاتِماً ٱلْأَصَمَّ كَانَ مِنْ أَصْحَابِ ٱلشَّقِيقِ ٱلْبَلْخِيِّ، رَحْمَةُ ٱللهِ تَعَالَى عَلَيْهِمَا، فَسَأَلَهُ يَوْماً قَالَ: صَاحَبْتَنِي مُنْذُ ثَلَاثِينَ سَنَةً مَا حَصَّلْتَ فِيهَا؟ قَالَ: حَصَّلْتُ ثَمَانِيَ فَوَائِدَ مِنَ ٱلْعِلْمِ وَهِيَ تَكْفِينِي مِنْهُ لِأَنِّي أَرْجُو خَلَاصِي وَنَجَاتِي فِيهَا. فَقَالَ شَقِيقٌ: مَا هِيَ؟ قَالَ حَاتِمٌ ٱلْأَصَمُّ:

[اَلْفَائِدَةُ ٱلْأُولَى] أَنِّي نَظَرْتُ إِلَى ٱلْخَلْقِ فَرَأَيْتُ لِكُلٍّ مِنْهُمْ مَحْبُوباً وَمَعْشُوقاً يُحِبُّهُ وَيَعْشَقُهُ، وَبَعْضُ ذٰلِكَ ٱلْمَحْبُوبِ يُصَاحِبُهُ إِلَى مَرَضِ ٱلْمَوْتِ، وَبَعْضُهُ إِلَى شَفِيرِ ٱلْقَبْرِ، ثُمَّ يَرْجِعُ كُلُّهُ وَيَتْرُكُهُ فَرِيداً وَحِيداً وَلَا يَدْخُلُ مَعَهُ فِي قَبْرِهِ مِنْهُمْ أَحَدٌ. فَتَفَكَّرْتُ وَقُلْتُ: أَفْضَلُ مَحْبُوبِ ٱلْمَرْءِ مَا يَدْخُلُ فِي قَبْرِهِ وَيُؤَانِسُهُ فِيهِ. فَمَا وَجَدْتُ غَيْرَ ٱلْأَعْمَالِ ٱلصَّالِحَةِ فَأَخَذْتُهَا مَحْبُوباً لِي لِتَكُونَ سِرَاجاً لِي فِي قَبْرِي وَتُؤَانِسَنِي فِيهِ وَلَا تَتْرُكَنِي فَرِيداً.

[اَلْفَائِدَةُ ٱلثَّانِيَةُ] أَنِّي رَأَيْتُ ٱلْخَلْقَ يَقْتَدُونَ بِأَهْوَائِهِمْ وَيُبَادِرُونَ إِلَى مُرَادَاتِ أَنْفُسِهِمْ، فَتَأَمَّلْتُ قَوْلَهُ تَعَالَى: «وَأَمَّا مَنْ

him who feared the station of his Lord, and kept the soul back from vain pleasure, the Garden is his abode."[30] I was certain that the Qur'ān is genuine truth, so I hurried to what my ego was opposed to, and I set to work combating it and restraining it from its pleasures, until it was satisfied with obedience to God the Glorified and Exalted, and it gave up.

'[The third useful lesson is that] I saw every individual in mankind exerting himself in accumulating the ephemeral things of the world, then clutching at them, laying hold on them, and I meditated on His saying (the Exalted), "What is in your possession dwindles and what is in God's possession is eternal."[31] So I sacrificed the gains I got from the world to God the Exalted, and I distributed them among the poor so that they might become a treasure for me with God the Exalted.

'[The fourth useful lesson is that] I saw that some of mankind believed their nobility and standing to be in the size of their nations and tribes, so they were conceited because of them. Others had the opinion that it lay in the wealth of their possessions, and the numerousness of sons, so they were proud of them. Some reckoned nobility and standing lay in forcibly acquiring the property of men, in tyrannizing them and spilling their blood. A group held that it consisted in wasting money, spending it lavishly, and squandering it. I meditated on His saying (the Exalted), "The noblest of you in the view of God is the most God-conscious of you."[32] So I chose God-consciousness, believing the Qur'ān to be accurate truth, and their opinion and evaluation utterly empty falsehood.

خَافَ مَقَامَ رَبِّهِ وَنَهَى ٱلنَّفْسَ عَنِ ٱلْهَوَى فَإِنَّ ٱلْجَنَّةَ هِيَ ٱلْمَأْوَىٰ.» وَتَيَقَّنْتُ أَنَّ ٱلْقُرْآنَ حَقٌّ صَادِقٌ، فَبَادَرْتُ إِلَى خِلَافِ نَفْسِي وَتَشَمَّرْتُ لِمُجَاهَدَتِهَا وَمَنْعِهَا عَنْ هَوَاهَا حَتَّى ٱرْتَاضَتْ لِطَاعَةِ ٱللهِ سُبْحَانَهُ وَتَعَالَى وَٱنْقَادَتْ.

[اَلْفَائِدَةُ ٱلثَّالِثَةُ] أَنِّي رَأَيْتُ كُلَّ وَاحِدٍ مِنَ ٱلنَّاسِ يَسْعَى فِي جَمْعِ حُطَامِ ٱلدُّنْيَا ثُمَّ يُمْسِكُهُ قَابِضاً يَدَهُ عَلَيْهِ. فَتَأَمَّلْتُ فِي قَوْلِهِ تَعَالَى: «مَا عِنْدَكُمْ يَنْفَدُ وَمَا عِنْدَ ٱللهِ بَاقٍ.» فَبَذَلْتُ مَحْصُولِي مِنَ ٱلدُّنْيَا لِوَجْهِ ٱللهِ تَعَالَى فَفَرَّقْتُهُ بَيْنَ ٱلْمَسَاكِينِ لِيَكُونَ ذُخْراً لِي عِنْدَ ٱللهِ تَعَالَى.

[اَلْفَائِدَةُ ٱلرَّابِعَةُ] أَنِّي رَأَيْتُ بَعْضَ ٱلْخَلْقِ ظَنَّ شَرَفَهُ وَعِزَّهُ فِي كَثْرَةِ ٱلْأَقْوَامِ وَٱلْعَشَائِرِ فَٱغْتَرَّ بِهِمْ. وَزَعَمَ آخَرُونَ أَنَّهُ فِي ثَرْوَةِ ٱلْأَمْوَالِ وَكَثْرَةِ ٱلْأَوْلَادِ فَٱفْتَخَرُوا بِهَا. وَحَسِبَ بَعْضُهُمُ ٱلشَّرَفَ وَٱلْعِزَّ فِي غَصْبِ أَمْوَالِ ٱلنَّاسِ وَظُلْمِهِمْ وَسَفْكِ دِمَائِهِمْ. وَٱعْتَقَدَتْ طَائِفَةٌ أَنَّهُ فِي إِتْلَافِ ٱلْمَالِ وَإِسْرَافِهِ وَتَبْذِيرِهِ. وَتَأَمَّلْتُ فِي قَوْلِهِ تَعَالَى: «إِنَّ أَكْرَمَكُمْ عِنْدَ ٱللهِ أَتْقَاكُمْ». فَٱخْتَرْتُ ٱلتَّقْوَى وَٱعْتَقَدْتُ أَنَّ ٱلْقُرْآنَ حَقٌّ صَادِقٌ وَظَنُّهُمْ وَحُسْبَانُهُمْ كُلُّهَا بَاطِلٌ زَائِلٌ.

'[The fifth useful lesson is that] I saw some people blaming others and some slandering others, and I found that that was through envy regarding money, fame and knowledge. So I meditated on His saying (the Exalted), "We distribute their subsistence amongst them in the life of the world,"[33] and I understood that the distribution was from God the Exalted in eternity, so I did not envy anyone and I was content with the distribution of God the Exalted.

'[The sixth useful lesson is that] I saw some people acting with hostility towards others due to some motive and cause. So I meditated on His saying (the Exalted), "Verily, Satan is an enemy to you, so take him as an enemy,"[34] and I understood that enmity towards anyone but Satan was not allowed.

'[The seventh useful lesson is that] I saw everyone striving in earnest, and working intensely in quest of their food and livelihood to the point that they thereby fell into what was dubious and banned, degrading themselves and lowering their worth. So I meditated on His statement (the Exalted), "No beast is on earth without its provision depending on God,"[35] and I understood that my provision depended on God the Exalted and that He had guaranteed it. So I occupied myself with worshipping Him and severed my hope from other than Him.

'[The eighth useful lesson is that] I saw everyone relying on something created—some on the dinar and dirham, some on wealth and property, some on their business and trade, and others on some similar created thing. So I meditated on His statement (the Exalted), "And whoso relies upon God—He is his sufficiency. Verily, God brings His command to pass. God has made a portion for everything."[36] So I relied on God, and He is my sufficiency and the most excellent trustee!'

[اَلْفَائِدَةُ الْخَامِسَةُ] أَنِّي رَأَيْتُ النَّاسَ يَذُمُّ بَعْضُهُمْ بَعْضاً وَيَغْتَابُ بَعْضُهُمْ بَعْضاً فَوَجَدْتُ ذٰلِكَ مِنَ الْحَسَدِ فِي الْمَالِ وَالْجَاهِ وَالْعِلْمِ. فَتَأَمَّلْتُ فِي قَوْلِهِ تَعَالَى: «نَحْنُ قَسَمْنَا بَيْنَهُمْ مَعِيشَتَهُمْ فِي الْحَيٰوةِ الدُّنْيَا.» فَعَلِمْتُ أَنَّ الْقِسْمَةَ كَانَتْ مِنَ اللهِ تَعَالَى فِي الْأَزَلِ، فَمَا حَسَدْتُ أَحَداً وَرَضِيتُ بِقِسْمَةِ اللهِ تَعَالَى .

[اَلْفَائِدَةُ السَّادِسَةُ] أَنِّي رَأَيْتُ النَّاسَ يُعَادِي بَعْضُهُمْ بَعْضاً لِغَرَضٍ وَسَبَبٍ. فَتَأَمَّلْتُ فِي قَوْلِهِ تَعَالَى: «إِنَّ الشَّيْطَانَ لَكُمْ عَدُوٌّ فَاتَّخِذُوهُ عَدُوّاً.» فَعَلِمْتُ أَنَّهُ لَا تَجُوزُ عَدَاوَةُ أَحَدٍ غَيْرِ الشَّيْطَانِ.

[اَلْفَائِدَةُ السَّابِعَةُ] أَنِّي رَأَيْتُ كُلَّ أَحَدٍ يَسْعَى بِجِدٍّ وَيَجْتَهِدُ بِمُبَالَغَةٍ لِطَلَبِ الْقُوتِ وَالْمَعَاشِ بِحَيْثُ يَقَعُ فِي شُبْهَةٍ وَحَرَامٍ وَيُذِلُّ نَفْسَهُ وَيُنْقِصُ قَدْرَهُ. فَتَأَمَّلْتُ فِي قَوْلِهِ تَعَالَى: «وَمَا مِنْ دَآبَّةٍ فِي الْأَرْضِ إِلَّا عَلَى اللهِ رِزْقُهَا.» فَعَلِمْتُ أَنَّ رِزْقِي عَلَى اللهِ تَعَالَى وَقَدْ ضَمِنَهُ. فَاشْتَغَلْتُ بِعِبَادَتِهِ وَقَطَعْتُ طَمَعِي عَمَّنْ سِوَاهُ.

[اَلْفَائِدَةُ الثَّامِنَةُ] أَنِّي رَأَيْتُ كُلَّ وَاحِدٍ مُعْتَمِداً عَلَى شَيْءٍ مَخْلُوقٍ. بَعْضُهُمْ عَلَى الدِّينَارِ وَالدِّرْهَمِ، وَبَعْضُهُمْ عَلَى الْمَالِ وَالْمُلْكِ، وَبَعْضُهُمْ عَلَى الْحِرْفَةِ وَالصِّنَاعَةِ، وَبَعْضُهُمْ عَلَى مَخْلُوقٍ مِثْلِهِ. فَتَأَمَّلْتُ فِي قَوْلِهِ تَعَالَى: «وَمَنْ يَتَوَكَّلْ عَلَى اللهِ فَهُوَ حَسْبُهُ إِنَّ اللهَ بَالِغُ أَمْرِهِ. قَدْ جَعَلَ اللهُ لِكُلِّ شَيْءٍ قَدْراً.» فَتَوَكَّلْتُ عَلَى اللهِ فَهُوَ حَسْبِي وَنِعْمَ الْوَكِيلُ.

Shaqīq said, 'May God the Exalted grant you success! I have examined the Torah, the Psalms, the Gospel, and the "Furqān" (i.e. the Qur'ān), and I discovered that the four books revolve around these eight useful lessons. Thus whoever acts on the basis of them, acts in accordance with these four books.'

أيها الولد

O disciple, you have understood from these two stories that you do not need extra learning. Now I will explain to you what is indispensable for the traveller on the way of truth.

Know that the traveller should have a master as a guide and instructor, to rid him of bad traits through his instruction and replace them with good ones. The significance of instruction is comparable to the work of the farmer who uproots thorn-bushes and removes weeds from the midst of the crops, so that his plants are in a proper condition, and his yield is brought to perfection.

The traveller must have a master to refine him and show him the way to God the Exalted. For God sent a messenger to His creatures in order to show the way to Him. And when he died—God bless him and give him peace—he appointed deputies in his place to show the way to God the Exalted. The criterion for the master who is fit to act as a representative of the Messenger of God (God's blessings and peace be upon him) is that he be knowledgeable. And yet not every knowledgeable man is fit for deputyship. I will explain to you some of his characteristics by way of generalization, lest everyone claim that he is a guide.

فَقَالَ شَقِيقٌ: وَفَّقَكَ ٱللّٰهُ تَعَالَى. إِنِّي قَدْ نَظَرْتُ ٱلتَّوْرَاةَ وَٱلزَّبُورَ وَٱلْإِنْجِيلَ وَٱلْفُرْقَانَ فَوَجَدْتُ ٱلْكُتُبَ ٱلْأَرْبَعَةَ تَدُورُ عَلَى هٰذِهِ ٱلْفَوَائِدِ ٱلثَّمَانِيَةِ. فَمَنْ عَمِلَ بِهَا كَانَ عَامِلاً بِهٰذِهِ ٱلْكُتُبِ ٱلْأَرْبَعَةِ.

أَيُّهَا ٱلْوَلَدُ

أَيُّهَا ٱلْوَلَدُ، قَدْ عَلِمْتَ مِنْ هَاتَيْنِ ٱلْحِكَايَتَيْنِ أَنَّكَ لَا تَحْتَاجُ إِلَى تَكْثِيرِ ٱلْعِلْمِ. وَٱلْآنَ أُبَيِّنُ لَكَ مَا يَجِبُ عَلَى سَالِكِ سَبِيلِ ٱلْحَقِّ:

إِعْلَمْ أَنَّهُ يَنْبَغِي لِلسَّالِكِ شَيْخٌ مُرْشِدٌ مُرَبٍّ لِيُخْرِجَ ٱلْأَخْلَاقَ ٱلسَّيِّئَةَ مِنْهُ بِتَرْبِيَتِهِ وَيَجْعَلَ مَكَانَهَا خُلُقاً حَسَناً. وَمَعْنَى ٱلتَّرْبِيَةِ يُشْبِهُ فِعْلَ ٱلْفَلَّاحِ ٱلَّذِي يَقْلَعُ ٱلشَّوْكَ وَيُخْرِجُ ٱلنَّبَاتَاتِ ٱلْأَجْنَبِيَّةَ مِنْ بَيْنِ ٱلزَّرْعِ لِيَحْسُنَ نَبَاتُهُ وَيَكْمُلَ رَيْعُهُ.

وَلَا بُدَّ لِلسَّالِكِ مِنْ شَيْخٍ يُؤَدِّبُهُ وَيُرْشِدُهُ إِلَى سَبِيلِ ٱللّٰهِ تَعَالَى. لِأَنَّ ٱللّٰهَ أَرْسَلَ لِلْعِبَادِ رَسُولاً لِلْإِرْشَادِ إِلَى سَبِيلِهِ. فَإِذَا ٱرْتَحَلَ صَلَّى ٱللّٰهُ عَلَيْهِ وَسَلَّمَ فَقَدْ خَلَّفَ ٱلْخُلَفَاءَ فِي مَكَانِهِ حَتَّى يُرْشِدُوا إِلَى ٱللّٰهِ تَعَالَى. وَشَرْطُ ٱلشَّيْخِ ٱلَّذِي يَصْلُحُ أَنْ يَكُونَ نَائِباً لِرَسُولِ ٱللّٰهِ، صَلَوَاتُ ٱللّٰهِ وَسَلَامُهُ عَلَيْهِ، أَنْ يَكُونَ عَالِماً. وَلَكِنْ مَا كُلُّ عَالِمٍ يَصْلُحُ لِلْخِلَافَةِ. وَإِنِّي أُبَيِّنُ لَكَ بَعْضَ عَلَامَاتِهِ عَلَى سَبِيلِ ٱلْإِجْمَالِ حَتَّى لَا يَدَّعِي كُلُّ أَحَدٍ أَنَّهُ مُرْشِدٌ.

So we say: it is someone who is averse to love of the world and love of fame; who has been the disciple of a person possessed of insight whose discipleship is part of a chain leading back to the Master of Messengers (God bless him and give him peace); who is proficient in disciplining his soul with little food, speech and sleep, and with much prayer, almsgiving, and fasting.

By his discipleship of that insightful master he has made into a way of life for himself proficiency in virtues such as patience, prayer, gratitude, reliance on God, certitude, contentment, self-composure, mildness, humility, knowledge, sincerity, modesty, fidelity, dignity, silence, deliberateness in acting, and suchlike. In consequence, he is a light among the lights of the Prophet (God bless him and give him peace), fit to be followed as an example.

However, finding the like of him is unusual—harder than red sulphur! Whoever is favoured by good fortune in finding a master such as we have mentioned, and the master accepts him, should venerate him outwardly and inwardly.

As for outward veneration—it is that he should not contend with him nor engage in argument with him over anything, even if he is aware of an error of his. He should not lay his prayer carpet down in front of him unless at the time of carrying out the formal prayer, and when he has finished he should remove it. He should not increase the number of optional prayers in his presence. He should do whatever task is commanded by the master as far as he can manage and is capable.

As for inward veneration—it is that everything he hears and receives from him externally should not be rejected by him internally, neither acts nor statements, lest he be charac-

فَنَقُولُ: مَنْ يُعْرِضُ عَنْ حُبِّ ٱلدُّنْيَا وَحُبِّ ٱلْجَاهِ، وَكَانَ قَدْ تَابَعَ لِشَخْصٍ بَصِيرٍ تَتَسَلْسَلُ مُتَابَعَتُهُ إِلَى سَيِّدِ ٱلْمُرْسَلِينَ، صَلَّى ٱللّٰهُ عَلَيْهِ وَسَلَّمَ، وَكَانَ مُحْسِناً رِيَاضَةَ نَفْسِهِ بِقِلَّةِ ٱلْأَكْلِ وَٱلْقَوْلِ وَٱلنَّوْمِ وَكَثْرَةِ ٱلصَّلَوَاتِ وَٱلصَّدَقَةِ وَٱلصَّوْمِ.

وَكَانَ بِمُتَابَعَتِهِ ذٰلِكَ ٱلشَّيْخَ ٱلْبَصِيرَ جَاعِلاً مَحَاسِنَ ٱلْأَخْلَاقِ لَهُ سِيرَةً كَٱلصَّبْرِ وَٱلصَّلَاةِ وَٱلشُّكْرِ وَٱلتَّوَكُّلِ وَٱلْيَقِينِ وَٱلْقَنَاعَةِ وَطُمَأْنِينَةِ ٱلنَّفْسِ وَٱلْحِلْمِ وَٱلتَّوَاضُعِ وَٱلْعِلْمِ وَٱلصِّدْقِ وَٱلْحَيَاءِ وَٱلْوَفَاءِ وَٱلْوَقَارِ وَٱلسُّكُونِ وَٱلتَّأَنِّي وَأَمْثَالِهَا، فَهُوَ إِذاً نُورٌ مِنْ أَنْوَارِ ٱلنَّبِيِّ، صَلَّى ٱللّٰهُ عَلَيْهِ وَسَلَّمَ، يَصْلُحُ لِلْإِقْتِدَاءِ بِهِ.

وَلَكِنَّ وُجودَ مِثْلِهِ نَادِرٌ أَعَزُّ مِنَ ٱلْكِبْرِيتِ ٱلْأَحْمَرِ. وَمَنْ سَاعَدَتْهُ ٱلسَّعَادَةُ فَوَجَدَ شَيْخاً كَمَا ذَكَرْنَا ، وَقَبِلَهُ ٱلشَّيْخُ، يَنْبَغِي أَنْ يَحْتَرِمَهُ ظَاهِراً وَبَاطِناً.

أَمَّا ٱحْتِرَامُ ٱلظَّاهِرِ فَهُوَ أَلَّا يُجَادِلَهُ وَلَا يَشْتَغِلَ بِٱلْإِحْتِجَاجِ مَعَهُ فِي كُلِّ مَسْأَلَةٍ، وَإِنْ عَلِمَ خَطَأَهُ. وَلَا يُلْقِيَ بَيْنَ يَدَيْهِ سَجَّادَتَهُ إِلَّا وَقْتَ أَدَاءِ ٱلصَّلَاةِ فَإِذَا فَرَغَ يَرْفَعُهَا. وَلَا يُكْثِرَ نَوَافِلَ ٱلصَّلَاةِ بِحَضْرَتِهِ. وَيَعْمَلَ مَا يَأْمُرُهُ ٱلشَّيْخُ مِنَ ٱلْعَمَلِ بِقَدْرِ وُسْعِهِ وَطَاقَتِهِ.

وَأَمَّا ٱحْتِرَامُ ٱلْبَاطِنِ فَهُوَ أَنَّ كُلَّ مَا يَسْمَعُ وَيَقْبَلُ مِنْهُ فِي ٱلظَّاهِرِ لَا يُنْكِرُهُ فِي ٱلْبَاطِنِ، لَا فِعْلاً وَلَا قَوْلاً، لِئَلَّا يَتَّسِمَ بِٱلنِّفَاقِ.

terized by hypocrisy. If he is unable, let him leave his company until his interior is consistent with his exterior. He should be on his guard against socializing with the wicked, so as to check the power of the demons among *jinn* and men in the recess of his heart, and so be rid of the taint of villainy, and at any rate he should choose poverty over wealth.

Then know that Sufism has two characteristics: correctness towards God the Exalted; and withdrawal from mankind. Whoever is correct towards God (Mighty and Majestic!), and masters his character with men, dealing with them mildly, is a Sufi. Correctness is to sacrifice the ego's pleasure to God's command (the Exalted). And excellence of character with men is not to get men to do what your ego wants, but to get your ego to do what they want, as long as they are not at odds with the Sharīʿa.

Next you questioned me about servanthood, and it is three things. The first of them is observing the ordinance of the Sharīʿa. The second of them is being satisfied with the divine decree, with predestination, and the fate allotted by God the Exalted. The third of them is rejecting the satisfaction of your ego, in seeking the satisfaction of God the Exalted.

You questioned me about reliance on God. It is that your creed about God the Exalted on what He has promised (and threatened),[A] come to be sincerely held. I mean you should believe that what has been predestined for you will inevitably reach you, even if all that is in the world tried to divert it from you. And what is not written will not come to you, even if the whole world helped you.

[A] *Waʿada* can mean both 'promise' and 'threaten', hence *al-waʿd* means 'the promise' and *al-waʿīd* 'the threat'.

وَإِنْ لَمْ يَسْتَطِعْ يَتْرُكْ صُحْبَتَهُ إِلَى أَنْ يُوافِقَ بَاطِنُهُ ظَاهِرَهُ. وَيَحْتَرِزُ عَنْ مُجَالَسَةِ صَاحِبِ ٱلسُّوءِ لِيَقْصُرَ وِلَايَةَ شَيَاطِينِ ٱلْجِنِّ وَٱلْإِنْسِ عَنْ صَحْنِ قَلْبِهِ، فَيُصَفَّى مِنْ لَوْثِ ٱلشَّيْطَنَةِ، وَعَلَى كُلِّ حَالٍ يَخْتَارُ ٱلْفَقْرَ عَلَى ٱلْغِنَى.

ثُمَّ ٱعْلَمْ أَنَّ ٱلتَّصَوُّفَ لَهُ خَصْلَتَانِ: ٱلْإِسْتِقَامَةُ مَعَ ٱللهِ تَعَالَى وَٱلسُّكُونُ عَنِ ٱلْخَلْقِ. فَمَنِ ٱسْتَقَامَ مَعَ ٱللهِ، عَزَّ وَجَلَّ، وَأَحْسَنَ خُلُقَهُ مَعَ ٱلنَّاسِ وَعَامَلَهُمْ بِٱلْحِلْمِ فَهُوَ صُوفِيٌّ. وَٱلْإِسْتِقَامَةُ أَنْ يَفْدِيَ حَظَّ نَفْسِهِ عَلَى أَمْرِ ٱللهِ تَعَالَى. وَحُسْنُ ٱلْخُلُقِ مَعَ ٱلنَّاسِ أَلَّا تَحْمِلَ ٱلنَّاسَ عَلَى مُرَادِ نَفْسِكَ، بَلْ تَحْمِلَ نَفْسَكَ عَلَى مُرَادِهِمْ، مَا لَمْ يُخَالِفُوا ٱلشَّرْعَ.

ثُمَّ إِنَّكَ سَأَلْتَنِي عَنِ ٱلْعُبُودِيَّةِ وَهِيَ ثَلَاثَةُ أَشْيَاءَ: أَحَدُهَا مُحَافَظَةُ أَمْرِ ٱلشَّرْعِ. وَثَانِيهَا ٱلرِّضَاءُ بِٱلْقَضَاءِ وَٱلْقَدَرِ وَقِسْمَةِ ٱللهِ تَعَالَى. وَثَالِثُهَا تَرْكُ رِضَاءِ نَفْسِكَ فِي طَلَبِ رِضَاءِ ٱللهِ تَعَالَى.

وَسَأَلْتَنِي عَنِ ٱلتَّوَكُّلِ وَهُوَ أَنْ يَسْتَحْكِمَ ٱعْتِقَادُكَ بِٱللهِ تَعَالَى فِيمَا وَعَدَ، يَعْنِي تَعْتَقِدُ أَنَّ مَا قُدِّرَ لَكَ سَيَصِلُ إِلَيْكَ لَا مَحَالَةَ وَإِنِ ٱجْتَهَدَ كُلُّ مَنْ فِي ٱلْعَالَمِ عَلَى صَرْفِهِ عَنْكَ، وَمَا لَمْ يُكْتَبْ لَنْ يَصِلَ إِلَيْكَ وَإِنْ سَاعَدَكَ جَمِيعُ ٱلْعَالَمِ.

You questioned me about sincerity. It is that all your deeds be for God the Exalted, and that your heart be not gladdened by men's praises nor that you care about their censure. Know that insincerity is produced by overestimating mankind. The cure for it is for you to see them as subject to omnipotence, and for you to reckon them as though inanimate objects, powerless to bestow ease or hardship, so you become free of insincerity towards them. As long as you reckon them as having control and free-will, insincerity will not keep away from you.

أيها الولد

O disciple, as for the rest of your questions—some are covered in my works, so look for them there. And putting others down in writing is an offence. Act in accordance with what you know for what you do not know to be unveiled to you.[A]

أيها الولد

O disciple, after today do not question me about what is difficult for you, except with 'the tongue of the heart', on account of His statement (the Exalted), 'And if they were patient till you emerged for them, it would be better for them.'[37] Accept the advice of Khaḍir (upon him be peace) when he said, 'Do not ask me about anything until I set about mentioning it to you.'[38] Do not rush so that you may reach the proper time when it will be unveiled to you and you will see it, 'I will show you My signs—so do not hurry Me!'[39] So do not question me prematurely, and be certain that you will not arrive without spiritual travel, on account of His statement (the Exalted), 'Have they not travelled the earth and considered?'[40]

أيها الولد

[A]Ghazālī is paraphrasing a prophetic Tradition: 'Whoso acts in accordance with what he knows, God bestows on him the knowledge of what he does not act on' (*man ʿamila bi-mā ʿalima awrathahu 'Llāhu taʿālā ʿilma mā lam yaʿmal*). Jarrāḥī, *Kashf al-khafā'*, vol. 2, p. 365, ḥadīth 2542.

وَسَأَلْتَنِي عَنِ ٱلْإِخْلَاصِ وَهُوَ أَنْ تَكُونَ أَعْمَالُكَ كُلُّهَا لِلّٰهِ تَعَالَى وَلَا يَرْتَاحَ قَلْبُكَ بِمَحَامِدِ ٱلنَّاسِ وَلَا تُبَالِي بِمَذَمَّتِهِمْ. وَٱعْلَمْ أَنَّ ٱلرِّيَاءَ يَتَوَلَّدُ مِنْ تَعْظِيمِ ٱلْخَلْقِ. وَعِلَاجُهُ أَنْ تَرَاهُمْ مُسَخَّرِيْنَ تَحْتَ ٱلْقُدْرَةِ وَتَحْسَبَهُمْ كَٱلْجَمَادَاتِ فِي عَدَمِ قُدْرَةِ إِيْصَالِ ٱلرَّاحَةِ وَٱلْمَشَقَّةِ لِتَتَخَلَّصَ مِنْ مُرَاءَاتِهِمْ. وَمَتَى تَحْسَبُهُمْ ذَوِي قُدْرَةٍ وَإِرَادَةٍ لَنْ يَبْعُدَ عَنْكَ ٱلرِّيَاءُ.

أَيُّهَا ٱلْوَلَدُ

أَيُّهَا ٱلْوَلَدُ، وَٱلْبَاقِي مِنْ مَسَائِلِكَ بَعْضُهَا مَسْطُورٌ فِي مُصَنَّفَاتِي فَاطْلُبْهُ ثَمَّةَ، وَكِتَابَةُ بَعْضِهَا حَرَامٌ. إِعْمَلْ أَنْتَ بِمَا تَعْلَمُ لِيَنْكَشِفَ لَكَ مَا لَمْ تَعْلَمْ.

أَيُّهَا ٱلْوَلَدُ

أَيُّهَا ٱلْوَلَدُ، بَعْدَ ٱلْيَوْمِ لَا تَسْأَلْنِي مَا أُشْكِلَ عَلَيْكَ إِلَّا بِلِسَانِ ٱلْجَنَانِ لِقَوْلِهِ تَعَالَى «وَلَوْ أَنَّهُمْ صَبَرُوا حَتَّىٰ تَخْرُجَ إِلَيْهِمْ لَكَانَ خَيْراً لَهُمْ.» وَٱقْبَلْ نَصِيحَةَ ٱلْخَضِرِ، عَلَيْهِ ٱلسَّلَامُ، حِينَ قَالَ: «فَلَا تَسْأَلْنِي عَنْ شَيْءٍ حَتَّىٰ أُحْدِثَ لَكَ مِنْهُ ذِكْراً.» وَلَا تَسْتَعْجِلْ حَتَّى تَبْلُغَ أَوَانَهُ فَيَنْكَشِفَ لَكَ وَتَرَاهُ «سَأُوْرِيكُمْ آيَتِي فَلَا تَسْتَعْجِلُونِ.» فَلَا تَسْأَلْنِي قَبْلَ ٱلْوَقْتِ، وَتَيَقَّنْ أَنَّكَ لَا تَصِلُ إِلَّا بِٱلسَّيْرِ، لِقَوْلِهِ تَعَالَى «أَوَ لَمْ يَسِيرُوا فِي ٱلْأَرْضِ فَيَنْظُرُوا.»

أَيُّهَا ٱلْوَلَدُ

O disciple—by God, if you travel you will see marvels at every stage! Persevere, for the main thing in this affair is perseverance. As Dhū 'l-Nūn al-Miṣrī (may God the Exalted be merciful to him) said to one of his disciples, 'If you can persevere, then come. If not, then do not engage in travesties of the Sufis.'[41]

أيها الولد

O disciple, I advise you about eight things. Accept them from me lest your knowledge becomes a liability for you on the Day of Resurrection. Accomplish four of them and give up four of them. As for the ones to give up:

[The first of them] is that you do not argue with anyone regarding any issue, insofar as you are able, since there is much that is harmful in it, and 'its evil is greater that its utility.'[A] For it is the origin of every ugly character trait, such as insincerity, envy, haughtiness, resentment, enmity, boastfulness and so on. Certainly, if an issue arises between you and an individual or a group, and your intention in regard to it is that the truth become known and not lost sight of, discussion is allowed you. However there are two indications of this intention. The first is that you make no distinction between the truth's being disclosed on your own tongue or that of someone else. The second is that discussion in private be preferable to you than in public.

[A]This echoes Q. II:219 on wine and gambling '*wa-ithmuhumā akbaru min naf*ʿ*ihimā.*'

أَيُّهَا ٱلْوَلَدُ، بِٱللهِ إِنْ تَسِرْ تَرَ ٱلْعَجَائِبَ فِي كُلِّ مَنْزِلٍ. وَٱبْذُلْ
رُوحَكَ فَإِنَّ رَأْسَ هٰذَا ٱلْأَمْرِ بَذْلُ ٱلرُّوحِ. كَمَا قَالَ ذُو ٱلنُّونِ
ٱلْمِصْرِيُّ، رَحِمَهُ ٱللهُ تَعَالَى، لِأَحَدِ تَلَامِذَتِهِ: إِنْ قَدَرْتَ عَلَى بَذْلِ
ٱلرُّوحِ فَتَعَالَ، وَإِلَّا فَلَا تَشْتَغِلْ بِتُرَّهَاتِ ٱلصُّوفِيَّةِ.

أَيُّهَا ٱلْوَلَدُ، إِنِّي أَنْصَحُكَ بِثَمَانِيَةِ أَشْيَاءَ. إِقْبَلْهَا مِنِّي لِئَلَّا يَكُونَ
عِلْمُكَ خَصْماً عَلَيْكَ يَوْمَ ٱلْقِيَامَةِ. تَعْمَلُ مِنْهَا أَرْبَعَةً، وَتَدَعُ مِنْهَا
أَرْبَعَةً. أَمَّا ٱللَّوَاتِي تَدَعُ:

[فَأَحَدُهَا] أَلَّا تُنَاظِرَ أَحَداً فِي مَسْأَلَةٍ مَا ٱسْتَطَعْتَ، لِأَنَّ فِيهَا
آفَاتٍ كَثِيرَةً. فَإِثْمُهَا أَكْبَرُ مِنْ نَفْعِهَا، إِذْ هِيَ مَنْبَعُ كُلِّ خُلُقٍ ذَمِيمٍ
كَٱلرِّيَاءِ وَٱلْحَسَدِ وَٱلْكِبْرِ وَٱلْحِقْدِ وَٱلْعَدَاوَةِ وَٱلْمُبَاهَاةِ وَغَيْرِهَا. نَعَمْ
لَوْ وَقَعَ مَسْأَلَةٌ بَيْنَكَ وَبَيْنَ شَخْصٍ أَوْ قَوْمٍ، وَكَانَتْ إِرَادَتُكَ فِيهَا أَنْ
يَظْهَرَ ٱلْحَقُّ وَلَا يَضِيعَ، جَازَ [لَكَ] ٱلْبَحْثُ لٰكِنْ لِتِلْكَ ٱلْإِرَادَةِ
عَلَامَتَانِ: إِحْدَاهُمَا أَلَّا تُفَرِّقَ بَيْنَ أَنْ يَنْكَشِفَ ٱلْحَقُّ عَلَى لِسَانِكَ
أَوْ عَلَى لِسَانِ غَيْرِكَ. وَٱلثَّانِيَةُ أَنْ يَكُونَ ٱلْبَحْثُ فِي ٱلْخَلَاءِ أَحَبَّ
إِلَيْكَ مِنْ أَنْ يَكُونَ فِي ٱلْمَلَإِ.

Listen—I will mention to you something useful at this juncture: understand that questioning about difficulties is [as it were] showing the sickness of the heart to a doctor, and replying to it is an attempt to cure this sickness. Know that the ignorant are the sick at heart, and the knowledgeable are the doctors. The man of inadequate knowledge is not expert in nursing, nor will the wholly knowledgeable man treat every patient. Instead he will treat whoever longs to get treatment and health. If the sickness is chronic or incurable, the expertise of the doctor in regard to it is to state that it is incurable, and he will not concern himself with treating it since it would waste his time.

Next, know that the disease of ignorance is of four kinds. The first of them is curable, and the rest incurable. As for what is incurable, the first is someone whose questioning or arguing is out of his envy and hate. Whenever you answer him with the best, clearest, or most evident reply, it only increases him in hate, hostility, and envy. The *modus operandi* is not to engage in replying to him. It has been said,

An end may be hoped for every hostility,
But his who was hostile to you through envy.

Thus you should turn away from him and leave him with his sickness. God the Exalted said, 'Turn away from whoever holds back from remembering Us and wants nothing but the

وَٱسْمَعْ إِنِّي أَذْكُرُ لَكَ هَاهُنَا فَائِدَةً، وَٱعْلَمْ أَنَّ ٱلسُّؤَالَ عَنِ ٱلْمُشْكِلَاتِ عَرْضُ مَرَضِ ٱلْقَلْبِ عَلَى ٱلطَّبِيبِ، وَٱلْجَوَابُ لَهُ سَعْيٌ لِإِصْلَاحِ مَرَضِهِ. وَٱعْلَمْ أَنَّ ٱلْجَاهِلِينَ ٱلْمَرْضَى قُلُوبُهُمْ، وَٱلْعُلَمَاءَ ٱلْأَطِبَّاءُ، وَٱلْعَالِمَ ٱلنَّاقِصَ لَا يُحْسِنُ ٱلْمُعَالَجَةَ، وَٱلْعَالِمَ ٱلْكَامِلَ لَا يُعَالِجُ كُلَّ مَرِيضٍ، بَلْ يُعَالِجُ مَنْ يَرْجُو قُبُولَ ٱلْمُعَالَجَةِ وَٱلصَّلَاحِ. وَإِذَا كَانَتِ ٱلْعِلَّةُ مُزْمِنَةً أَوْ عَقِيماً لَا تَقْبَلُ ٱلْعِلَاجَ فَحَذَاقَةُ ٱلطَّبِيبِ فِيهِ أَنْ يَقُولَ هٰذَا لَا يَقْبَلُ ٱلْعِلَاجَ فَلَا تَشْتَغِلْ فِيهِ بِمُدَاوَاتِهِ لِأَنَّ فِيهِ تَضْيِيعَ ٱلْعُمُرِ.

ثُمَّ ٱعْلَمْ أَنَّ مَرَضَ ٱلْجَهْلِ عَلَى أَرْبَعَةِ أَنْوَاعٍ: أَحَدُهَا يَقْبَلُ ٱلْعِلَاجَ وَٱلْبَاقِي لَا يَقْبَلُ. أَمَا أَلَّذِي لَا يَقْبَلُ ٱلْعِلَاجَ فَأَحَدُهَا مَنْ كَانَ سُؤَالُهُ وَٱعْتِرَاضُهُ عَنْ حَسَدِهِ وَبُغْضِهِ، فَكُلَّمَا تُجِيبُهُ بِأَحْسَنِ ٱلْجَوَابِ وَأَفْصَحِهِ وَأَوْضَحِهِ، فَلَا يَزِيدُ لَهُ ذَلِكَ إِلَّا بُغْضاً وَعَدَاوَةً وَحَسَداً. فَٱلطَّرِيقُ أَلَّا تَشْتَغِلَ بِجَوَابِهِ، فَقَدْ قِيلَ:

كُلُّ ٱلْعَدَاوَةِ قَدْ تُرْجَى إِزَالَتُهَا
إِلَّا عَدَاوَةَ مَنْ عَادَاكَ عَنْ حَسَدِ

فَيَنْبَغِي أَنْ تُعْرِضَ عَنْهُ وَتَتْرُكَهُ مَعَ مَرَضِهِ. قَالَ ٱللّٰهُ تَعَالَى: «فَأَعْرِضْ عَنْ مَنْ تَوَلَّىٰ عَنْ ذِكْرِنَا وَلَمْ يُرِدْ إِلَّا ٱلْحَيَوٰةَ ٱلدُّنْيَا.»

life of the world.'[42] The envious man in whatever he says and does, sets fire to the crop of his deeds,[43] as the Prophet (upon him be peace) said, 'Envy devours good deeds as fire devours wood.'[44]

The second has foolishness as his sickness, and he too is incurable. As Jesus said (upon him be peace), 'Verily, I was not incapable of bringing the dead to life, but I was incapable of curing the fool.'[45] This is someone who spent a small time in pursuit of learning, studying something in the way of non-revelatory and revelatory knowledge, so out of his stupidity he interrogates and queries the great scholar who has passed his life in the non-revelatory and revelatory sciences, and this idiot in his ignorance thinks that what is a problem for him is also problematic for the great scholar. Since he does not know [even] this much, his questioning is due to his foolishness, and you should not engage in answering him.

The third is someone asking for guidance, and everything he does not understand in the discussion of the great scholars is put down [by him] to the shortcomings in his own knowledge, and his questioning is to learn. However he is unintelligent and does not grasp realities. Thus you should not engage in answering him either, as God's Messenger (God bless him and give him peace) said, 'We, the assemblies of the prophets, have been commanded to address men in proportion to their intellects.'[46]

As for the sickness which is curable—it is that of someone asking for guidance, [who is] intelligent, understanding, not overwhelmed by envy, anger, the love of reputation, prestige and wealth, being a seeker of the Straight Path,[47] and

وَٱلْحَسُودُ بِكُلِّ مَا يَقُولُ وَيَفْعَلُ يُوقِدُ ٱلنَّارَ فِي زَرْعِ عَمَلِهِ، كَمَا قَالَ ٱلنَّبِيُّ، عَلَيْهِ ٱلسَّلَامُ: أَلْحَسَدُ يَأْكُلُ ٱلْحَسَنَاتِ كَمَا تَأْكُلُ ٱلنَّارُ ٱلْحَطَبَ.

وَٱلثَّانِي أَنْ تَكُونَ عِلَّتُهُ مِنَ ٱلْحَمَاقَةِ وَهُوَ أَيْضاً لَا يَقْبَلُ ٱلْعِلَاجَ، كَمَا قَالَ عِيسَى، عَلَيْهِ ٱلسَّلَامُ: إِنِّي مَا عَجَزْتُ عَنْ إِحْيَاءِ ٱلْمَوْتَى وَقَدْ عَجَزْتُ عَنْ مُعَالَجَةِ ٱلْأَحْمَقِ. وَذٰلِكَ رَجُلٌ يَشْتَغِلُ بِطَلَبِ ٱلْعِلْمِ زَمَناً قَلِيلاً وَيَتَعَلَّمُ شَيْئًا مِنَ ٱلْعِلْمِ ٱلْعَقْلِيِّ وَٱلشَّرْعِيِّ فَيَسْأَلُ وَيَعْتَرِضُ مِنْ حَمَاقَتِهِ عَلَى ٱلْعَالِمِ ٱلْكَبِيرِ ٱلَّذِي مَضَى عُمْرُهُ فِي ٱلْعُلُومِ ٱلْعَقْلِيَّةِ وَٱلشَّرْعِيَّةِ. وَهٰذَا ٱلْأَحْمَقُ لَا يَعْلَمُ وَيَظُنُّ أَنَّ مَا أُشْكِلَ عَلَيْهِ هُوَ أَيْضًا مُشْكِلٌ عَلَى ٱلْعَالِمِ ٱلْكَبِيرِ. فَإِذَا لَمْ يَعْلَمْ هٰذَا ٱلْقَدْرَ يَكُونُ سُؤَالُهُ مِنَ ٱلْحَمَاقَةِ. فَيَنْبَغِي أَلَّا تَشْتَغِلَ بِجَوَابِهِ.

وَٱلثَّالِثُ أَنْ يَكُونَ مُسْتَرْشِدًا وَكُلُّ مَا لَا يَفْهَمُ مِنْ كَلَامِ ٱلْأَكَابِرِ يُحْمَلُ عَلَى قُصُورِ فَهْمِهِ وَكَانَ سُؤَالُهُ لِلْإِسْتِفَادَةِ، لٰكِنْ يَكُونُ بَلِيدًا لَا يُدْرِكُ ٱلْحَقَائِقَ، فَلَا يَنْبَغِي ٱلْإِشْتِغَالُ بِجَوَابِهِ أَيْضًا، كَمَا قَالَ رَسُولُ ٱللهِ، صَلَّى ٱللهُ عَلَيْهِ وَسَلَّمَ: نَحْنُ مَعَاشِرَ ٱلْأَنْبِيَاءِ أُمِرْنَا أَنْ نُكَلِّمَ ٱلنَّاسَ عَلَى قَدْرِ عُقُولِهِمْ.

وَأَمَّا ٱلْمَرَضُ أَلَّذِي يَقْبَلُ ٱلْعِلَاجَ فَهُوَ أَنْ يَكُونَ مُسْتَرْشِدًا عَاقِلًا فَهِمًا، لَا يَكُونُ مَغْلُوبَ ٱلْحَسَدِ وَٱلْغَضَبِ وَحُبِّ ٱلشُّهْرَةِ وَٱلْجَاهِ وَٱلْمَالِ، وَيَكُونُ طَالِبَ ٱلطَّرِيقِ ٱلْمُسْتَقِيمِ، وَلَمْ يَكُنْ سُؤَالُهُ

whose questioning and querying are not out of envy, obstinacy or desire to test. This man is curable, and it is permissible to engage in a reply to his question, in fact replying to him is obligatory for you.

[The second thing] to give up is: That you are on your guard against becoming a preacher or admonisher for it involves much harm, unless you first 'practice what you preach', then preach it to people. Think of what was said to Jesus (upon him be peace), 'O Son of Mary! Preach to your soul, and if it learns its lesson, preach to people—otherwise show humility before your Lord.'[48]

If you are put to the test with this occupation, be careful of two traits: First is pretentiousness in talking, by way of idioms, allusions, outbursts, verses and poems—for God the Exalted detests the pretentious. The pretentious and excessive man exhibits inward decadence and the indifference of his heart. The idea of admonition is for the worshipper to recollect the fire of the hereafter and his own remissness in the service of the Creator, to consider his past life which he has spent in what did not concern him, and consider what difficulties lie before him such as the absence of firmness of faith in his life's final moments, the nature of his state in the clasps of the Angel of Death, and whether he will be capable of answering Munkar and Nakīr,[49] that he worry about his state during the Resurrection and its episodes, and whether he will cross the Bridge safely or tumble into the abyss.[50] The recollection of these things should remain in his heart and upset his apathy. To foment these fires and lament these calamities is termed 'admonition'.

وَٱعْتِرَاضُهُ عَنْ حَسَدٍ وَتَعَنُّتٍ وَٱمْتِحَانٍ. وَهٰذَا يَقْبَلُ ٱلْعِلَاجَ فَيَجُوزُ أَنْ تَشْتَغِلَ بِجَوَابِ سُؤَالِهِ، بَلْ يَجِبُ عَلَيْكَ إِجَابَتُهُ.

[وَٱلثَّانِي] مِمَّا تَدَعُ هُوَ أَنْ تَحْذَرَ مِنْ أَنْ تَكُونَ وَاعِظاً وَمُذَكِّراً لِأَنَّ فِيهِ آفَةً كَثِيرَةً، إِلَّا أَنْ تَعْمَلَ بِمَا تَقُولُ أَوَّلاً ثُمَّ تَعِظَ بِهِ ٱلنَّاسَ. فَتَفَكَّرْ فِيمَا قِيلَ لِعِيسَى، عَلَيْهِ ٱلسَّلَامُ: يَا ٱبْنَ مَرْيَمَ عِظْ نَفْسَكَ فَإِنِ ٱتَّعَظَتْ فَعِظِ ٱلنَّاسَ وَإِلَّا فَٱسْتَحِ مِنْ رَبِّكَ.

وَإِنِ ٱبْتُلِيتَ بِهٰذَا ٱلْعَمَلِ فَٱحْتَرِزْ عَنْ خَصْلَتَيْنِ: اَلْأُولَى عَنِ ٱلتَّكَلُّفِ فِي ٱلْكَلَامِ بِٱلْعِبَارَاتِ وَٱلْإِشَارَاتِ وَٱلطَّامَّاتِ وَٱلْأَبْيَاتِ وَٱلْأَشْعَارِ، لِأَنَّ ٱللهَ تَعَالَى يُبْغِضُ ٱلْمُتَكَلِّفِينَ، وَٱلْمُتَكَلِّفُ ٱلْمُتَجَاوِزُ عَنِ ٱلْحَدِّ يَدُلُّ عَلَى خَرَابِ ٱلْبَاطِنِ وَغَفْلَةِ ٱلْقَلْبِ. وَمَعْنَى ٱلتَّذْكِيرِ أَنْ يَذْكُرَ ٱلْعَبْدُ نَارَ ٱلْآخِرَةِ وَتَقْصِيرَ نَفْسِهِ فِي خِدْمَةِ ٱلْخَالِقِ، وَيَتَفَكَّرَ فِي عُمُرِهِ ٱلْمَاضِي ٱلَّذِي أَفْنَاهُ فِيمَا لَا يُعِينُهُ، وَيَتَفَكَّرَ فِيمَا بَيْنَ يَدَيْهِ مِنَ ٱلْعَقَبَاتِ مِنْ عَدَمِ سَلَامَةِ ٱلْإِيمَانِ فِي ٱلْخَاتِمَةِ، وَكَيْفِيَّةِ حَالِهِ فِي قَبْضِ مَلَكِ ٱلْمَوْتِ وَهَلْ يَقْدِرُ عَلَى جَوَابِ مُنْكَرٍ وَنَكِيرٍ، وَيَهْتَمَّ بِحَالِهِ فِي ٱلْقِيَامَةِ وَمَوَاقِفِهَا، وَهَلْ يَعْبُرُ عَنِ ٱلصِّرَاطِ سَالِماً أَمْ يَقَعُ فِي ٱلْهَاوِيَةِ؟ وَيَسْتَمِرُّ ذِكْرُ هَذِهِ ٱلْأَشْيَاءِ فِي قَلْبِهِ فَيُزْعِجُهُ عَنْ قَرَارِهِ. فَغَلَيَانُ هٰذِهِ ٱلنِّيرَانِ وَنَوْحَةُ هٰذِهِ ٱلْمَصَائِبِ يُسَمَّى تَذْكِيراً.

Informing mankind and apprising them of these things, warning them of their remissness and negligence, making them see the defects of their egos, so that the heat of these fires impinges on the congregation, and the calamities disturb them so that they make amends for their past lives as far as possible, and they are distressed by the days passed in disobedience to God the Exalted: all this in this way is termed 'preaching'.

It is as if you saw that a flood bore down on an individual's house with him and his family inside, and you said, 'Look out! Look out! Run from the flood!' In these circumstances does your heart long for you to give the owner of the house your message with pretentious expressions, anecdotes and allusions? It is completely repugnant to you! The situation of the preacher is like this and he should give them up.

The second trait is that your effort in your preaching should not be for the people in your congregation to roar or show hysteria and tear at their clothes, so that it is said, 'What a gathering that was!' For all this is worldliness, and that is produced by indifference. Rather your zealous intention must be to lead men from the world to the hereafter, from recalcitrance to obedience, from acquisitiveness to renunciation, from stinginess to generosity, from doubt to certainty, from indifference to vigilance, and from illusion to God-consciousness. You should evoke in them love of the afterlife and loathing for the world. You should teach them about worship and asceticism. Do not allow them to be complacent due to the kindness of God the

وَإِعْلَامُ ٱلْخَلْقِ وَإِطْلَاعُهُمْ عَلَى هٰذِهِ ٱلْأَشْيَاءِ وَتَنْبِيهُهُمْ عَلَى تَقْصِيرِهِمْ وَتَفْرِيطِهِمْ وَتَبْصِيرُهُمْ بِعُيُوبِ أَنْفُسِهِمْ لِتَمَسَّ حَرَارَةُ هَذِهِ ٱلنِّيرَانِ أَهْلَ ٱلْمَجْلِسِ وَتُجْزِعُهُمْ تِلْكَ ٱلْمَصَائِبُ لِيَتَدَارَكُوا ٱلْعُمُرَ ٱلْمَاضِيَ بِقَدْرِ ٱلطَّاقَةِ وَيَتَحَسَّرُوا عَلَى ٱلْأَيَّامِ ٱلْخَالِيَةِ فِي غَيْرِ طَاعَةِ ٱللهِ تَعَالَى: هَذِهِ ٱلْجُمْلَةُ عَلَى هٰذَا ٱلطَّرِيقِ تُسَمَّى وَعْظاً.

كَمَا لَوْ رَأَيْتَ أَنَّ ٱلسَّيْلَ قَدْ هَجَمَ عَلَى دَارِ أَحَدٍ، وَكَانَ هُوَ وَأَهْلُهُ فِيهَا، فَتَقُولُ: ٱلْحَذَرَ ٱلْحَذَرَ، فِرُّوا مِنَ ٱلسَّيْلِ. وَهَلْ يَشْتَهِي قَلْبُكَ فِي هٰذِهِ ٱلْحَالَةِ أَنْ تُخْبِرَ صَاحِبَ ٱلدَّارِ خَبَرَكَ بِتَكَلُّفِ ٱلْعِبَارَاتِ وَٱلنُّكَتِ وَٱلْإِشَارَاتِ؟ فَلَا تَشْتَهِي ٱلْبَتَّةَ، فَكَذٰلِكَ حَالُ ٱلْوَاعِظِ، فَيَنْبَغِي أَنْ يَجْتَنِبَهَا.

وَٱلْخَصْلَةُ ٱلثَّانِيَةُ أَلَّا تَكُونَ هِمَّتُكَ فِي وَعْظِكَ أَنْ يَنْعَرَ ٱلْخَلْقُ فِي مَجْلِسِكَ أَوْ يُظْهِرُوا ٱلْوَجْدَ وَيَشُقُّوا ٱلثِّيَابَ لِيُقَالَ: نِعْمَ ٱلْمَجْلِسُ هٰذَا. لِأَنَّ كُلَّهُ مَيْلٌ لِلدُّنْيَا، وَهُوَ يَتَوَلَّدُ مِنَ ٱلْغَفْلَةِ. بَلْ يَنْبَغِي أَنْ يَكُونَ عَزْمُكَ وَهِمَّتُكَ أَنْ تَدْعُوَ ٱلنَّاسَ مِنَ ٱلدُّنْيَا إِلَى ٱلْآخِرَةِ وَمِنَ ٱلْمَعْصِيَةِ إِلَى ٱلطَّاعَةِ وَمِنَ ٱلْحِرْصِ إِلَى ٱلزُّهْدِ وَمِنَ ٱلْبُخْلِ إِلَى ٱلسَّخَاءِ وَمِنَ ٱلشَّكِّ إِلَى ٱلْيَقِينِ وَمِنَ ٱلْغَفْلَةِ إِلَى ٱلْيَقْظَةِ وَمِنَ ٱلْغُرُورِ إِلَى ٱلتَّقْوَى، وَتُحَبِّبَ إِلَيْهِمُ ٱلْآخِرَةَ وَتُبَغِّضَ إِلَيْهِمُ ٱلدُّنْيَا، وَتُعَلِّمَهُمْ عِلْمَ ٱلْعِبَادَةِ وَٱلزُّهْدِ، وَلَا تُغِرَّهُمْ بِكَرَمِ ٱللهِ

Exalted (Glorious and Majestic!) and His mercy, since predominating in their natures is disinclination from the path of the Law, drive in what displeases God the Exalted, and getting tripped up by bad morals. Put fear into their hearts, alarm them and put them on their guard regarding the dangers they will face. Perhaps their inward qualities will be transformed, and their outward behaviour exchanged—'acquisitiveness' and an 'appetite' for obedience, and for repentance from disobedience, will appear.

This then is the right way to preach and advise, and all preaching not thus is a curse upon both speaker and listener. Nay, it is said that [the former] is a ghoul, a demon who sweeps men off the path and destroys them, and they must run from him, since this speaker will wreak havoc on their religion the like of which Satan himself cannot. It is incumbent on whoever has the wherewithal and capability, to get him down from pulpits and prevent him from sermonizing, for this is part of 'enjoining good and forbidding evil.'[51]

[The third thing] to give up is that you have nothing to do with princes and rulers, nor see them, because the spectacle of them, gatherings with them and socialising with them are a serious danger. If you are put to the test by this, avoid praising them and complimenting them, for God the Exalted is angered if a wrongdoer or tyrant is praised, and whoever prays for their long life wants God to be disobeyed on His earth.

تَعَالَى، عَزَّ وَجَلَّ، وَرَحْمَتِهِ، لِأَنَّ ٱلْغَالِبَ فِي طِبَاعِهِمْ ٱلزَّيْغُ عَنْ مَنْهَجِ ٱلشَّرْعِ وَٱلسَّعْيُ فِيمَا لَا يَرْضَى ٱللّٰهُ تَعَالَى بِهِ وَٱلْإِسْتِغْثَارُ بِٱلْأَخْلَاقِ ٱلرَّدِيَّةِ. فَأَلْقِ فِي قُلُوبِهِمْ ٱلرُّعْبَ وَرَوِّعْهُمْ وَحَذِّرْهُمْ عَمَّا يَسْتَقْبِلُونَ مِنَ ٱلْمَخَاوِفِ، لَعَلَّ صِفَاتِ بَاطِنِهِمْ تَتَغَيَّرُ وَمُعَامَلَةَ ظَاهِرِهِمْ تَتَبَدَّلُ وَيَظْهَرُ ٱلْحِرْصُ وَٱلرَّغْبَةُ فِي ٱلطَّاعَةِ وَٱلرُّجُوعِ عَنِ ٱلْمَعْصِيَةِ.

وَهٰذَا طَرِيقُ ٱلْوَعْظِ وَٱلنَّصِيحَةِ، وَكُلُّ وَعْظٍ لَا يَكُونُ هٰكَذَا فَهُوَ وَبَالٌ عَلَى مَنْ قَالَ وَسَمِعَ. بَلْ قِيلَ: إِنَّهُ غُولٌ وَشَيْطَانٌ يَذْهَبُ بِٱلْخَلْقِ عَنِ ٱلطَّرِيقِ وَيُهْلِكُهُمْ، فَيَجِبُ عَلَيْهِمْ أَنْ يَفِرُّوا مِنْهُ لِأَنَّ مَا يُفْسِدُ هٰذَا ٱلْقَائِلُ مِنْ دِينِهِمْ لَا يَسْتَطِيعُ بِمِثْلِهِ ٱلشَّيْطَانُ. وَمَنْ كَانَتْ لَهُ يَدٌ وَقُدْرَةٌ يَجِبُ عَلَيْهِ أَنْ يُنْزِلَهُ عَنْ مَنَابِرِ ٱلْمَوَاعِظِ وَيَمْنَعَهُ عَمَّا بَاشَرَ فَإِنَّهُ مِنْ جُمْلَةِ ٱلْأَمْرِ بِٱلْمَعْرُوفِ وَٱلنَّهْيِ عَنِ ٱلْمُنْكَرِ.

[وَٱلثَّالِثُ] مِمَّا تَدَعُ أَلَّا تُخَالِطَ ٱلْأُمَرَاءَ وَٱلسَّلَاطِينَ وَلَا تَرَاهُمْ، لِأَنَّ رُؤْيَتَهُمْ وَمُجَالَسَتَهُمْ وَمُخَالَطَتَهُمْ آفَةٌ عَظِيمَةٌ. وَلَوْ ٱبْتُلِيتَ بِهَا، دَعْ عَنْكَ مَدْحَهُمْ وَثَنَاءَهُمْ لِأَنَّ ٱللّٰهَ تَعَالَى يَغْضَبُ إِذَا مُدِحَ ٱلْفَاسِقُ وَٱلظَّالِمُ. وَمَنْ دَعَا لِطُولِ بَقَائِهِمْ فَقَدْ أَحَبَّ أَنْ يُعْصَى ٱللّٰهُ فِي أَرْضِهِ.

[The fourth thing] to give up is to accept nothing of the benefaction of princes nor their presents, even if you know they were acquired legitimately. For expecting it from them degrades religion, in that sycophancy, partiality for them and complicity in their tyranny are produced by it. All this is corruption in religion. The least of its harm is that when you receive their donations and profit from their material possessions, you like them, and whoever likes an individual would prefer him to have a long life span, unavoidably. Preferring the survival of the tyrant constitutes a desire for the creatures of God the Exalted [to continue] to suffer tyranny, and a desire for the world's ruination. What is worse than this for religion and our final ends? Beware! Beware that the demons' suggestions, or some people's talk to you does not deceive you to the effect that 'the best and most appropriate thing is for you to receive the money from them and distribute it amongst the poor and beggars, for they are wasting it in dissolute living and disobedience and your spending it on helpless people is better than their spending it.' For the Accursed One has severed many people's necks by these whisperings! We have mentioned this in the *Revival of the Sciences*, so look for it there.[52]

As for the four things which you must do: [The first is] that you make your relations with God the Exalted such that were a servant of yours to behave thus with you, you would be content with him and not weary of liking him, nor get angry. Whatever would dissatisfy you for yourself on the part of this hypothetical servant of yours, should dissatisfy you also for God the Exalted, and He is actually your Lord!

[وَٱلرَّابِعُ] مِمَّا تَدَعُ أَلَّا تَقْبَلَ شَيْئًا مِنْ عَطَاءِ ٱلْأُمَرَاءِ وَهَدَايَاهُمْ، وَإِنْ عَلِمْتَ أَنَّهَا مِنَ ٱلْحَلَالِ. لِأَنَّ ٱلْمَطْمَعَ مِنْهُمْ يُفْسِدُ ٱلدِّينَ، لِأَنَّهُ يَتَوَلَّدُ مِنْهُ ٱلْمُدَاهَنَةُ وَمُرَاعَاةُ جَانِبِهِمْ وَٱلْمُوافَقَةُ فِي ظُلْمِهِمْ. وَهٰذَا كُلُّهُ فَسَادٌ فِي ٱلدِّينِ. وَأَقَلُّ مَضَرَّتِهِ أَنَّكَ إِذَا قَبِلْتَ عَطَايَاهُمْ وَٱنْتَفَعْتَ مِنْ دُنْيَاهُمْ أَحْبَبْتَهُمْ، وَمَنْ أَحَبَّ أَحَداً يُحِبُّ طُولَ عُمُرِهِ وَبَقَائِهِ بِٱلضَّرُورَةِ، وَفِي مَحَبَّةِ بَقَاءِ ٱلظَّالِمِ إِرَادَةُ [لِدَوَامِ] ٱلظُّلْمِ عَلَى عِبَادِ ٱللهِ تَعَالَى وَإِرَادَةُ خَرَابِ ٱلْعَالَمِ. فَأَيُّ شَيْءٍ يَكُونُ أَضَرَّ مِنْ هٰذَا لِلدِّينِ وَٱلْعَاقِبَةِ؟ وَإِيَّاكَ إِيَّاكَ أَنْ يَخْدَعَكَ ٱسْتِهْوَاءُ ٱلشَّيَاطِينِ أَوْ قَوْلُ بَعْضِ ٱلنَّاسِ لَكَ بِأَنَّ ٱلْأَفْضَلَ وَٱلْأَوْلَى أَنْ تَأْخُذَ ٱلدِّينَارَ وَٱلدِّرْهَمَ مِنْهُمْ وَتُفَرِّقَهُمَا بَيْنَ ٱلْفُقَرَاءِ وَٱلْمَسَاكِينِ فَإِنَّهُمْ يُنْفِقُونَ فِي ٱلْفِسْقِ وَٱلْمَعْصِيَةِ، وَإِنْفَاقُكَ عَلَى ضُعَفَاءِ ٱلنَّاسِ خَيْرٌ مِنْ إِنْفَاقِهِمْ، فَإِنَّ ٱللَّعِينَ قَدْ قَطَعَ أَعْنَاقَ كَثِيرٍ مِنَ ٱلنَّاسِ بِهٰذِهِ ٱلْوَسْوَسَةِ، وَقَدْ ذَكَرْنَاهُ فِي إِحْيَاءِ ٱلْعُلُومِ فَٱطْلُبْهُ ثَمَّةَ.

وَأَمَّا ٱلْأَرْبَعَةُ ٱلَّتِي يَنْبَغِي لَكَ أَنْ تَفْعَلَهَا: [فَٱلْأَوَّلُ] أَنْ تَجْعَلَ مُعَامَلَتَكَ مَعَ ٱللهِ تَعَالَى بِحَيْثُ لَوْ عَامَلَ مَعَكَ بِهَا عَبْدُكَ تَرْضَى بِهَا مِنْهُ وَلَا يَضِيقُ خَاطِرُكَ عَلَيْهِ وَلَا تَغْضَبُ، وَٱلَّذِي لَا تَرْضَى لِنَفْسِكَ مِنْ عَبْدِكَ ٱلْمَجَازِيِّ فَلَا تَرْضَ أَيْضاً لِلهِ تَعَالَى وَهُوَ سَيِّدُكَ ٱلْحَقِيقِيُّ.

[The second is] whenever you interact with people, deal with them as you would wish yourself to be dealt with by them, for a worshipper's faith is incomplete until he wants for other people what he wants for himself.

[The third is] if you read or study knowledge, your knowledge must improve your heart and purge your ego—just as if you learned that your life would only last another week, inevitably you would not spend it in learning about law, ethics, jurisprudence, scholastic theology and suchlike, because you would know that these sciences would be inadequate for you. Instead, you would occupy yourself with inspecting your heart, discerning the features of your personality, giving worldly attachments a wide berth, purging yourself of ugly traits, and you would occupy yourself in adoring God the Exalted, worshipping Him, and acquiring good qualities. And not a day or night passes for [any] worshipper without his death during it being a possibility!

أيها الولد

O disciple, listen to another statement from me, and think about it to find salvation. If you were notified that the ruler would be coming to you on a visit in a week's time, I know that during this period you would be occupied with nothing but putting in order what you knew his glance would fall on of your clothing, your person, house, furnishings and so on. Now think what it is I am hinting at, for you are intelli-

[وَٱلثَّانِي] كُلَّمَا عَمِلْتَ بِٱلنَّاسِ ٱجْعَلْهُ كَمَا تَرْضَى لِنَفْسِكَ مِنْهُمْ لِأَنَّهُ لَا يَكْمُلُ إِيمَانُ عَبْدٍ حَتَّى يُحِبَّ لِسَائِرِ ٱلنَّاسِ مَا يُحِبُّ لِنَفْسِهِ.

[وَٱلثَّالِثُ] إِذَا قَرَأْتَ ٱلْعِلْمَ أَوْ طَالَعْتَهُ يَنْبَغِي أَنْ يَكُونَ عِلْمُكَ يُصْلِحُ قَلْبَكَ وَيُزَكِّي نَفْسَكَ، كَمَا لَوْ عَلِمْتَ أَنَّ عُمْرَكَ مَا يَبْقَى غَيْرَ أُسْبُوعٍ، فَبِالضَّرُورَةِ لَا تَشْتَغِلُ فِيهَا بِعِلْمِ ٱلْفِقْهِ وَٱلْأَخْلَاقِ وَٱلْأُصُولِ وَٱلْكَلَامِ وَأَمْثَالِهَا، لِأَنَّكَ تَعْلَمُ أَنَّ هٰذِهِ ٱلْعُلُومَ لَا تُغْنِيكَ. بَلْ تَشْتَغِلُ بِمُرَاقَبَةِ ٱلْقَلْبِ وَمَعْرِفَةِ صِفَاتِ ٱلنَّفْسِ وَٱلْإِعْرَاضِ عَنْ عَلَائِقِ ٱلدُّنْيَا وَتُزَكِّي نَفْسَكَ عَنِ ٱلْأَخْلَاقِ ٱلذَّمِيمَةِ وَتَشْتَغِلُ بِمَحَبَّةِ ٱللهِ تَعَالَى وَعِبَادَتِهِ وَٱلْإِتِّصَافِ بِٱلْأَوْصَافِ ٱلْحَسَنَةِ، وَلَا يَمُرُّ عَلَى عَبْدٍ يَوْمٌ وَلَيْلَةٌ إِلَّا وَيُمْكِنُ أَنْ يَكُونَ مَوْتُهُ فِيهِ.

أَيُّهَا ٱلْوَلَدُ، إِسْمَعْ مِنِّي كَلَامًا آخَرَ وَتَفَكَّرْ فِيهِ حَتَّى تَجِدَ خَلَاصًا: لَوْ أَنَّكَ أُخْبِرْتَ أَنَّ ٱلسُّلْطَانَ بَعْدَ أُسْبُوعٍ يَجِيئُكَ زَائِرًا، فَأَنَا أَعْلَمُ أَنَّكَ فِي تِلْكَ ٱلْمُدَّةِ لَا تَشْتَغِلُ إِلَّا بِإِصْلَاحِ مَا عَلِمْتَ أَنَّ نَظَرَ ٱلسُّلْطَانِ سَيَقَعُ عَلَيْهِ مِنَ ٱلثِّيَابِ وَٱلْبَدَنِ وَٱلدَّارِ وَٱلْفِرَاشِ وَغَيْرِهَا، وَٱلْآنَ تَفَكَّرْ إِلَى مَا أَشَرْتُ بِهِ فَإِنَّكَ فَهِمٌ، وَٱلْكَلَامُ ٱلْفَرْدُ

gent. A single word is enough for someone clever. The Messenger of God said (upon him be blessings and peace), 'God will not look upon your forms, nor upon your deeds, but He will look into your hearts and your intentions.'[53] If you want the science of the states of the heart, look at the *Revival* and other works of mine.[54] This science is an individual obligation, while others are a collective obligation,[55] except the amount [needed] for obligations to God the Exalted to be performed.[A] And He it is who will grant you success in acquiring it.

[The fourth is that] you should not stock up more of the world's produce than is adequate for one year, as the Messenger of God (upon him be blessings and peace) used to arrange this for one of his wives, saying, 'O God, make the sustenance of Muḥammad's family enough!'[56] And he used not to arrange this for all his wives, but he used to arrange it for the one in whose heart he knew was a weakness. As for whoever [of his wives] was confident—he used not to arrange more than one or half a day's sustenance for her.

أيها الولد

O disciple, I have addressed the things you asked for in this discourse, and you must carry them out, and do not forget me in this—to mention me in your devout supplications! As for the prayer which you requested from me, look for it amongst the supplications in collections of authentic Traditions and recite this prayer during all the moments you have, in particular as a supererogation after your formal prostrations:

[A]The sentence contains an ellipsis. The thought is that Sufism ('the science of the states of the heart') is a responsibility for every adult Muslim. All other religious sciences are the responsibility of the scholars (i.e. a collective obligation) *except* insofar as the knowledge of certain details of such sciences is necessary for every adult Muslim in fulfilling his or her individual obligations towards God.

يَكْفِي ٱلْكَيِّس. قَالَ رَسُولُ ٱللهِ، عَلَيْهِ ٱلصَّلاَةُ وَٱلسَّلاَمُ: إِنَّ ٱللهَ لَا يَنْظُرُ إِلَى صُوَرِكُمْ وَلَا إِلَى أَعْمَالِكُمْ وَلَكِنْ يَنْظُرُ إِلَى قُلُوبِكُمْ وَنِيَّاتِكُمْ. وَإِنْ أَرَدْتَ عِلْمَ أَحْوَالِ ٱلْقَلْبِ فَٱنْظُرْ إِلَى ٱلْإِحْيَاءِ وَغَيْرِهِ مِنْ مُصَنَّفَاتِي. وَهٰذَا ٱلْعِلْمُ فَرْض عَيْنٍ، وَغَيْرُهُ فَرْض كِفَايَةٍ، إِلَّا مِقْدَارَ مَا يُؤَدَّى بِهِ فَرَائِضَ ٱللهِ تَعَالَى، وَهُوَ يُوَفِّقُكَ حَتَّى تُحَصِّلَهُ.

[وَٱلرَّابِعُ] أَلَّا تَجْمَعَ مِنَ ٱلدُّنْيَا أَكْثَرَ مِنْ كِفَايَةِ سَنَةٍ، كَمَا كَانَ رَسُولُ ٱللهِ، عَلَيْهِ ٱلصَّلاَةُ وَٱلسَّلاَمُ، يُعِدُّ ذٰلِكَ لِبَعْضِ حُجُرَاتِهِ وَقَالَ: اَللّٰهُمَّ ٱجْعَلْ قُوتَ آلِ مُحَمَّدٍ كَفَافاً. وَلَمْ يَكُنْ يُعِدُّ ذٰلِكَ لِكُلِّ حُجُرَاتِهِ بَلْ كَانَ يُعِدُّهُ لِمَنْ عَلِمَ أَنَّ فِي قَلْبِهَا ضَعْفاً. وَأَمَّا مَنْ كَانَتْ صَاحِبَةَ يَقِينٍ فَمَا كَانَ يُعِدُّ لَهَا أَكْثَرَ مِنْ قُوتِ يَوْمٍ أَوْ نِصْفٍ.

أَيُّهَا ٱلْوَلَدُ، إِنِّي كَتَبْتُ فِي هَذَا ٱلْفَصْلِ مُلْتَمَسَاتِكَ فَيَنْبَغِي لَكَ أَنْ تَعْمَلَ بِهَا وَلَا تَنْسَانِي فِيهِ مِنْ أَنْ تَذْكُرَنِي فِي صَالِحِ دُعَائِكَ. وَأَمَّا ٱلدُّعَاءُ ٱلَّذِي سَأَلْتَ مِنِّي فَٱطْلُبْهُ مِنْ دَعَوَاتِ ٱلصِّحَاحِ، وَٱقْرَأْ هَذَا ٱلدُّعَاءَ فِي جَمِيعِ أَوْقَاتِكَ خُصُوصاً أَعْقَابَ صَلَوَاتِكَ:

O God, I beg Thee in regard to grace for its completeness, in regard to protection for its permanence, in regard to mercy for its totality, in regard to wellbeing for its realization, in regard to livelihood for the most plentiful, in regard to life for the most happy, in regard to beneficence for the most perfect, in regard to favour for the most inclusive, in regard to generosity for the most sweet, and in regard to gentleness for the most intimate.

O God, be for us and do not be against us! O God, conclude our lives with happiness, and make our hopes abundantly real, unite our mornings and evenings in wellbeing, and entrust our destiny and future state to Thy mercy, pour the vessel of Thy forgiveness over our sins,[A] grant us the correction of our faults, make God-consciousness our provision, and make our exertion to be for Thy religion, and our trust and our confidence to be in Thee.

O God, set us upon the path of righteousness, protect us in the world from causes of regret on the Day of Resurrection, lighten the weight of our sins, endow us with the way of life of the godly, restrain us from and avert from us the evil of the wicked, and release our necks and the necks of our fathers, mothers, brothers, and sisters from hellfire, by Thy Mercy, Thou Infinitely Precious, Thou Ever-Forgiving, Thou Bountiful One, Thou Veiler of sins, Thou Omniscient and Omnipotent!

O God, O God, O God! By Thy Mercy, Thou Most Merciful of the Merciful, Thou First of all and Last of all, Thou Mighty Lord of Power, Thou who hast mercy on the needy, Thou Most Merciful of the Merciful, there is no god but Thou, glory be to Thee: I am a sinner! God bless our liege lord Muḥammad, all his Family and Companions, and praise belongs to God, the Lord of the Worlds.

[A] As well as *dhunūb* (sins), *dhanūb* would signify 'a full bucket', and so we have a possible paronomasia here: God's vessel (*sijāl*) filling-up our *dhanūb*.

أَللّٰهُمَّ إِنِّي أَسْأَلُكَ مِنَ ٱلنِّعْمَةِ تَمَامَهَا، وَمِنَ ٱلْعِصْمَةِ دَوَامَهَا، وَمِنَ ٱلرَّحْمَةِ شُمُولَهَا، وَمِنَ ٱلْعَافِيَةِ حُصُولَهَا، وَمِنَ ٱلْعَيْشِ أَرْغَدَهُ، وَمِنَ ٱلْعُمُرِ أَسْعَدَهُ، وَمِنَ ٱلْإِحْسَانِ أَتَمَّهُ، وَمِنَ ٱلْإِنْعَامِ أَعَمَّهُ، وَمِنَ ٱلْفَضْلِ أَعْذَبَهُ، وَمِنَ ٱللُّطْفِ أَقْرَبَهُ.

اَللّٰهُمَّ كُنْ لَنَا وَلَا تَكُنْ عَلَيْنَا. اَللّٰهُمَّ ٱخْتِمْ بِٱلسَّعَادَةِ آجَالَنَا، وَحَقِّقْ بِٱلزِّيَادَةِ آمَالَنَا، وَأَقْرِنْ بِٱلْعَافِيَةِ غُدُوَّنَا وَآصَالَنَا، وَٱجْعَلْ إِلَى رَحْمَتِكَ مَصِيرَنَا وَمَآلَنَا ، وَٱصْبُبْ سِجَالَ عَفْوِكَ عَلَى ذُنُوبِنَا، وَمُنَّ عَلَيْنَا بِإِصْلَاحِ عُيُوبِنَا، وَٱجْعَلِ ٱلتَّقْوَى زَادَنَا، وَفِي دِينِكَ ٱجْتِهَادَنَا، وَعَلَيْكَ تَوَكُّلَنَا وَٱعْتِمَادَنَا.

اَللّٰهُمَّ ثَبِّتْنَا عَلَى نَهْجِ ٱلْإِسْتِقَامَةِ، وَأَعِذْنَا فِي ٱلدُّنْيَا مِنْ مُوجِبَاتِ ٱلنَّدَامَةِ يَوْمَ ٱلْقِيَامَةِ ، وَخَفِّفْ عَنَّا ثِقْلَ ٱلْأَوْزَارِ، وَٱرْزُقْنَا عِيشَةَ ٱلْأَبْرَارِ، وَٱكْفِنَا وَٱصْرِفْ عَنَّا شَرَّ ٱلْأَشْرَارِ، وَأَعْتِقْ رِقَابَنَا وَرِقَابَ آبَائِنَا وَأُمَّهَاتِنَا وَإِخْوَانِنَا وَأَخَوَاتِنَا مِنَ ٱلنَّارِ، بِرَحْمَتِكَ يَا عَزِيزُ يَا غَفَّارُ، يَا كَرِيمُ يَا سَتَّارُ، يَا عَلِيمُ يَا جَبَّارُ.

يَا ٱللّٰهُ يَا ٱللّٰهُ يَا ٱللّٰهُ، بِرَحْمَتِكَ يَا أَرْحَمَ ٱلرَّاحِمِينَ، وَيَا أَوَّلَ ٱلْأَوَّلِينَ، وَيَا آخِرَ ٱلْآخِرِينَ، وَيَا ذَا ٱلْقُوَّةِ ٱلْمَتِينِ، وَيَا رَاحِمَ ٱلْمَسَاكِينِ، وَيَا أَرْحَمَ ٱلرَّاحِمِينَ، لَا إِلٰهَ إِلَّا أَنْتَ سُبْحَانَكَ إِنِّي كُنْتُ مِنَ ٱلظَّالِمِينَ. وَصَلَّى ٱللّٰهُ عَلَى سَيِّدِنَا مُحَمَّدٍ وَآلِهِ وَصَحْبِهِ أَجْمَعِينَ، وَٱلْحَمْدُ لِلّٰهِ رَبِّ ٱلْعَالَمِينَ.

Notes

[1] Q. VII:128. The translation of *al-muttaqīn* as 'the God-conscious' and *taqwā* as 'God-consciousness' follows Muḥammad Asad, *The Message of the Qur'ān, passim.*

[2] Muslim, *Dhikr*, 73; Abū Dāūd, *Witr*, 32; Tirmidhī *Daʿawāt*, 68.

[3] Compare the Tradition '*Min ḥusni Islāmi 'l-mar'i tarkuhu mā lā yaʿnīhi.*' Cf. Ibn Māja, *Fitan*, 12.

[4] Jarrāḥī, *Kashf al-khafā' wa-muzīl 'l-ilbās*, vol. 1, p. 145, ḥadīth 376; also Hindī, *Kanz al-ʿummāl*, vol. 10, p. 187, ḥadīth 28977.

[5] See p. xxx.

[6] Q. LIII:39.

[7] Q. XVIII:110.

[8] Q. IX:95.

[9] Q. XVIII:107–108.

[10] Q. XIX:59.

[11] Bukhārī, *Īmān*, 1, 2; *Tafsīr Sūrat al-Baqara*, 30; Muslim, *Īmān*, 19–22; Tirmidhī, *Īmān*, 3; Nasā'ī, *Īmān*, 13.

[12] Q. VII:56.

[13] Tirmidhī, *Qiyāma*, 25. This Tradition is the basis for the Sufi practice called *muḥāsabat al-nafs*. See *EI*[2], VII, p. 465.

[14] Tirmidhī, *Qiyāma*, 25; Ibn Māja, *Zuhd*, 31; Ibn Ḥanbal, 4.124.

[15] Allusion to Q. XII:53.

[16] Jarrāḥī, *Kashf al-khafā'*, vol. 2, p. 77, ḥadīth 1731.

[17] An apocryphal text. But compare Mat. 6:1–6.

[18] Q. XXXII:12.

[19] Q. LXXXIX:28.

[20] Bukhārī, *Manāqib al-anṣār*, 12; Muslim, *Faḍā'il al-ṣaḥāba*, 123–125; Tirmidhī, *Manāqib*, 50; Ibn Māja, *Muqaddima*, 11; Ibn Ḥanbal, 3.234.

[21] Q. VII:179.

[22] Q. VII:50.

[23] Bukhārī, *Faḍā'il al-ṣaḥāba*, 21.

[24] Ibn Māja, *Iqāma*, 174.

[25] Q. XVII:79.

[26] Q. LI:18.

[27] Q. III:17. The quotation is a description of God's servants (*ʿibād*).

[28] Hindī, *Kanz al-ʿummāl* vol. 12, p. 335, ḥadīth 35285.

[29] Compare this to the Tradition, '*Aṣliḥū al-dunyā wa-ʿmalū li-ākhiratikum ka-annakum tamūtūna ghadan.*' Hindī, *Kanz al-ʿummāl* vol. 15, p. 546, ḥadīth 42111.

[30] Q. LXXIX:40–41.
[31] Q. XVI:96.
[32] Q. XLIX:13.
[33] Q. XLIII:32.
[34] Q. XXXV:6.
[35] Q. XI:6.
[36] Q. LXV:3.
[37] Q. XLIX:5.
[38] Q. XVIII:70.
[39] Q. XXI:37.
[40] Q. XXX:9.
[41] See Introduction p. xxvii
[42] Q. LIII:29.
[43] Variant reading: *ʿilmihi*.
[44] Ibn Māja, *Zuhd*, 22; Abū Dāūd, *Adab*, 44.
[45] An apocryphal text.
[46] Bukhārī, *ʿIlm*, 1.225
[47] Compare Q. I:6.
[48] An apocryphal text.
[49] See appendix, 'Munkar and Nakīr'.
[50] The Bridge (*ṣirāṭ, jisr*) over the abyss of hell is mentioned in eschatological Traditions, e.g. Bukhārī, *Adhān*, 129; Muslim, *Īmān*, 302.
[51] Following Q. III:104, 114, etc.
[52] See the extensive discussion of this subject in *K. al-Ḥalāl wa 'l-ḥarām*, Book XIV of the *Revival*: *Fī idrārāt al-salāṭīn*. Ghazālī, *Iḥyā'*, vol. 2, p. 135ff.
[53] Muslim, *Birr*, 32; Ibn Māja, *Zuhd*, 9; Ibn Ḥanbal, 2.285, 539.
[54] See especially *K. Sharḥ ʿajā'ib al-qalb*, Book XXI of the *Revival*. Ghazālī, *Iḥyā'*, vol. 3, p. 2ff. For a summary in English of Book XXI see Appendix III 'The Wonders of the Heart' in T. J. Winter, *Al-Ghazālī on Disciplining the Soul*, pp. 233–243.
[55] See introduction, p. xx.
[56] Bukhārī, *Raqaq*, 17; Muslim, *Zuhd*, 18, 19; *Zakāt*, 126; Tirmidhī, *Zuhd*, 38; Ibn Māja, *Zuhd*, 9; Ibn Ḥanbal, 2.232, 446, 481.

Appendix
Persons cited in the text

ʿABD ALLĀH IBN ʿUMAR (d. 73 [693/4])—20. A Companion of the Prophet and a major transmitter of Traditions. The son of the Caliph ʿUmar Ibn al-Khaṭṭāb with whom he had embraced Islam, he was famed for piety and moral qualities. He fought at the Battle of the Ditch aged fifteen. Such was his scrupulousness in religion that reports were collected on his manner of dress and behaviour. The caliphate was offered him three times but he turned it down, choosing to dedicate himself to learning for which he was renowned. It is said he rejected the office of *qāḍi*, so anxious was he about any misinterpretation of the law. Died as a result of a wound apparently unintentionally delivered by one of the soldiers of al-Ḥajjāj. (*EI*² I.53–4 [L. Veccia Vaglieri]; ʿAsqalānī, *Iṣāba*, II. 338–341.)

ABŪ BAKR AL-ṢIDDĪQ, ibn Abī Quḥāfa al-Taymī (d. 13 [634])—xxix, 18. The first of the four Righteous Caliphs and the Prophet's chief adviser. He had been a merchant before Islam and had been respected for his knowledge of genealogy. He bought and manumitted Bilāl and ʿĀmir ibn Fuhayra after their persecution by the pagans in Mecca. He personally accompanied the Prophet on the *Hijra* in 622. Father of the Prophet's wife ʿĀ'isha. Involved in his two-year caliphate in suppressing a wave of apostasy in Yemen, the Banū Ḥanīfa in the Yamāma, the tribes of Asad and Ghaṭafān, and the tribe of Tamīm. When Abū Bakr dispatched Khālid ibn al-Walīd to Iraq, he effectively initiated the great wave of Islamic conquests. He died in Medina after an illness. (*EI*[2] I.109–111 [W. Montgomery Watt].)

ʿALĪ IBN ABĪ ṬĀLIB (d. 40 [660])—xvii, xxx, xxxv, 12. Ranked with Khadīja as the first to embrace Islam, ʿAlī was was the cousin and son-in-law of the Prophet through his marriage to Fāṭima. On the death of ʿUthmān, he became the fourth of the Righteous Caliphs. He is also the first Imām of the Shīʿa. Possibly the foremost spiritual authority in Islam after the Prophet who, after describing himself as the city of knowledge, said ʿAlī was its gate. A great warrior of Islam about whom the angel Gabriel said, 'No knight if not ʿAlī!' (*lā fatā illā ʿAlī*). Slain by the Khārijite ʿAbd al-Raḥmān ibn Muljam al-Murādī after a troubled caliphate. (*EI*[2] I.381–6 [L. Veccia Vaglieri]; Ibn ʿAbd al-Barr, *Istīʿāb*, III.26–27.)

DHŪ'L-NŪN al-Miṣrī, Thawbān (d. 245 [859/60])—xxvii, 42. A famous Sufi of the earlier period, of Nubian stock. He was a disciple of Saʿdūn in Cairo. Dhū 'l-Nūn was said to have been the first to formulate systematically the Sufi doctrine of the states and stations (*aḥwāl, maqāmāt*). He was an early proponent of a properly gnostic Sufism, describing the saints as 'those who contemplate God in their hearts, so that God reveals Himself to them in a way in which He is not revealed to any others in the world'. He was an alchemist, and works by him on this subject as well as magic have survived. Attacked by the Muʿtazila for asserting the uncreatedness of the Qur'ān. Also attacked by ʿAbd Allāh ibn ʿAbd al-Ḥakam for public Sufi-preaching. Arrested and released by the Caliph al-Mutawakkil. (*EI*[2] II.242 [M. Smith]; Qushayrī, *Risāla*, I.58–61.)

AL-ḤASAN al-Baṣrī (d. 110 [728/9])—xxxi, 10, 12, 18. One of the most famous of the 'successors' (*tābiʿūn*). Born in Medina, as a young man he took part in the campaigns of conquest in Eastern Iran and then became a preacher in Baṣra. His sermons which have survived in fragments are considered amongst the best examples of early Arabic prose. His sanctity and eloquence attracted many to his sermons and his name occurs in many Sufi chains (*silsila*). (*EI*[2] III.247–8 [H. Ritter]; Iṣfahānī, *Ḥilyat al-awliyā'*, II.131–161.)

ḤĀTIM AL-AṢAMM al-Balkhī (d. 237 [851/2])—xxxii, 28. An important Sufi of the earlier period and cited often in the *Risāla al-Qushayriyya*. He was known as the 'Luqmān of this community', famous for his asceticism and otherworldliness, preoccupations reflected in what is quoted of him. He visited Baghdad where he met Aḥmad ibn Ḥanbal. Died at Wāshgird near Resht in Transoxiana. (Iṣfahānī, *Ḥilyat al-awliyā'*, VIII.73–84.)

AL-JUNAYD, Abū 'l-Qāsim ibn Muḥammad (d. 298 [910/11])—x, xxx, 6. Native of Baghdad, Junayd was nephew and disciple of Sarī al-Saqaṭī. He associated with Ḥārith al-Muḥāsibī and with him became an exponent of the Sufism of 'sobriety' (*ṣaḥw*). The honorary titles he acquired reflect the respect he attained in that capacity: 'Lord of the Sect' (*sayyid al-ṭā'ifa*), 'Peacock of the Mendicants' (*ta'ūs al-fuqarā'*), and 'Director of the Spiritual Directors' (*shaykh al-mashāyikh*). His *rasā'il* have in large part survived in a single, though fragmentary, manuscript (GALS, I.354–5). His style is involved; he was among the first Sufis to discuss the doctrine of 'passing away' (*fanā'*). Famous for having been one of the Sufis to have signed the document calling for the execution of Manṣūr al-Ḥallāj. In law, he followed the school of Abū Thawr, and his gatherings were attended not only by Sufis, but also jurists, theologians, and philosophers. (*EI*[2] II.600 [A. J. Arberry]; A. H. Abdel-Kader, *The Life, Personality and Writings of al-Junayd*.)

AL-KHAḌIR—40. An immortal sage, usually understood to be a prophet, and related in some respects to the figure Utnapishtim in the Gilgamesh story. He is green (*khaḍir*) because immortal. He is identified normally with the mysterious 'servant of God' encountered by Moses (Q. XVIII: 65–82). In this Qur'ānic story Khaḍir tells Moses he may accompany him as long as he does not challenge anything he does, but after successive incomprehensible deeds, Moses cannot help protesting. Before parting, Khaḍir explains the wisdom of his actions. In this respect Khaḍir is a Qur'ānic paradigm for certain manifestations of Sufism such as the Malāmiyya. (*EI*² IV.902–5 [A. J. Wensick].)

LUQMĀN—22. A pre-Islamic Arab sage mentioned in the Qur'ān, understood to have been granted enormous longevity as a reward for his piety. Thus as well as being styled 'the Wise' (*al-ḥakīm*), he was also known in ancient Arab lore as the 'Long-lived' (*al-muʿammar*). Qur'ān XXXI is named after him; in it he counsels his son with the repeated expression 'My dear son' (*yā bunayya*). Hence he is regularly associated in the Islamic tradition with salutary maxims, so, for example, Maydānī's collection of proverbs contains many attributed to Luqmān. (*EI*² V.811–3 [B. Heller-[N. A. Stillman]]; Maydānī, *Majmaʿ al-amthāl, passim*.)

MUNKAR AND NAKĪR—48. Names of two angels who in Muslim belief examine souls in the intermediate, i.e., purgatorial state after death but before Resurrection. They are in other words the executors of what is called the 'Punishment of the Grave' (*ʿadhāb al-qabr*), a decisive eschatological doctrine of Sunnism. The *Waṣiyyat Abī Ḥanīfa* mentions them by name (art. 18, 19), and similarly *al-Fiqh al-akbar* II (art. 23). The Karrāmiyya sect taught that Munkar and Nakīr are to be identified with the two guardian angels of every individual during their life (See Q. L:17). While their names only explicitly occur in the Tradition, they are implicitly referred to in Qur'ān VI:93, VIII:50, and XLVII:27.

SA'D IBN MU'ĀDH al-Awsī (d. 5 [626])—18. Companion of the Prophet and leader of the Banū 'Abd al-Ashhal who were part of the great Medinan clan of al-Aws. Converted before the *Hijra* of the Prophet and made standard-bearer at the Battle of Badr. On the Prophet's arrival in Medina, he became one of his strongest supporters. Sa'd was mortally wounded at the Battle of the Ditch (*Khandaq*), and, as head of Aws, was then entrusted by the Prophet with the judgment of the Banū Qurayẓa, a Jewish tribe associated with Aws, who had conspired during the battle with Islam's pagan enemies. (*EI*[2] VIII.697 [W. Montgomery Watt].)

SHAQĪQ AL-BALKHĪ, al-Azdī (d. 194 [809/10])—xxxii, 28. Sufi ascetic. One of the famous *shaykhs* of Khorāsān, a direct disciple of Ibrāhīm ibn Adham, and possibly the first to speak on the theory of mystical states (*aḥwāl*), he was also a warrior and died in battle in Transoxiana. Met Mūsā al-Kāẓim (seventh Imām of the Shī'a) in 149/766–7 in Qādisiyya and recognised him as a saint (*walī Allāh*) and among their elite (*min al-abdāl*). He is mentioned in the *Risāla al-Qushayriyya*. (Qushayrī, *Risāla*, I.85–87; Iṣfahānī, *Ḥilyat al-awliyā'*, VIII.58–73.)

AL-SHIBLĪ, ibn Jaḥdar (d. 334 [945/6])—xxxii, 26. Mālikī Sufi born in Baghdad into a Transoxianan family. After working as a government official till the age of forty, he became an ascetic and member of the Sufi circles of the capital. He occupies an intermediary position between Ḥallāj and Junayd. He denied Ḥallāj, who had been his friend, before the vizier, even supposedly accusing him from beneath the scaffold. Later, however, he affected insanity and spent time in a Baghdad asylum. His theopathic utterances (*shaṭaḥāt*) and strange acts figure in classical Sufi literature. (*EI* IV.360 [L. Massignon]; Qushayrī, *Risāla*, I.159–160.)

SUFYĀN AL-THAWRĪ, ibn Saʿīd (d. 161 [777/8])—20. Theologian and ascetic, also a traditionist who was taught Traditions from his father. He was amongst the first to commit the great number of Traditions in his knowledge to writing, and is sometimes even ranked above Mālik ibn Anas. He is credited with founding a defunct strongly Tradition-based legal school (*madhhab*). He was offered numerous official positions under the Umayyads, but declined to take up any. The Sufis assert he was one of their own and Abū Naṣr al-Sarrāj in the *Lumaʿ* cites him as evidence of Sufism's non-innovated status. (*EI* IV.500 [M. Plessner]; Iṣfahānī, *Ḥilyat al-awliyā'*, VI.356–393, VII.3–144.)

Bibliography

Abdel-Kader, A. H. *The Life, Personality and Writings of al-Junayd*. London, 1977.

Asad, Muhammad. *The Message of the Qur'ān*. Bristol, 2003.

ʿAsqalānī, Ibn Ḥajar, al-. *al-Iṣāba fī tamyīz al-ṣaḥāba*. Cairo, 1359/1940.

Bouyges, Maurice. *Essai de chronologie des œuvres de al-Ghazālī (Algha-zel)*. Ed. and revised by M. Allard. Beirut, 1959.

Brockelmann, C. *Geschichte der arabischen Litteratur*. 2nd ed. Leiden, 1943–1949.

———*Geschichte der arabischen Litteratur. Supplement*. Leiden, 1937–1942.

Buchman, D. *The Niche of Lights*. See Ghazālī, al-, *The Niche of Lights*.

Davidson, H. A. *Alfarabi, Avicenna, and Averroes, on Intellect*. Oxford, 1992.

Descartes, René. *Meditations on First Philosophy, With Selections from the Objections and Replies*. Ed. John Cottingham. Cambridge, 1996.

Ess, Josef van, 'Scepticism in Islamic Religious Thought'. *Al-Abḥāth*, 21 (1968), pp. 1–19.

Ethé, Hermann. *Catalogue of Persian Manuscripts in the Library of the India Office*. Revised and completed by Edward Edwards. Oxford, 1903-1937.

Frank, R. *Al-Ghazālī and the Ashʿarite School*. Durham and London, 1994.

Ghazālī, Abū Ḥāmid Muḥammad, al-. *Faḍā'iḥ al-Bāṭiniyya wa-faḍā'il al-Mustaẓhiriyya*. Ed. ʿAbd al-Raḥmān Badawī. Cairo, 1383/1964.

———*Iḥyā' ʿulūm al-dīn*. Beirut, n.d. 5 vols.

———*The Incoherence of the Philosophers*. Tr. and ed. Michael E. Marmura. Provo, 1997. The Arabic of this edition is modified from that of Maurice Bouyges.

———*al-Iqtiṣād fī 'l-iʿtiqād*. Eds. Ibrāhīm Āgāh Çubukçu and Hüseyin Ātay. Ankara, 1962.

———*K. Khulāṣat al-taṣnīf fī 'l-taṣawwuf*. Ar. trans. from Persian by Muḥammad Amīn al-Kurdī. Cairo, 1327/1909.

———*Mīzān al-ʿamal*. Ed. Sulaymān Dunyā. Cairo, 1383/1964.

———*al-Munqidh min al-ḍalāl wa 'l-mūṣil ilā Dhī 'l-ʿizzati wa 'l-jalāl*. Ar. ed. and French trans. by Farīd Jabre. Beirut, 1389/1969.

———*al-Mustaṣfā min ʿilm al-uṣūl*. Ed. Muḥammad Abū 'l-ʿAlā. Cairo, 1391/1971.

———*The Niche of Lights*. Tr. and ed. D. Buchman. Provo, 1998.

———*Tahāfut al-falāsifa*. Ed. M. Bouyges. Beirut, 1927.

Gianotti, T. J. *Al-Ghazālī's Unspeakable Doctrine of the Soul: Unveiling the Esoteric Psychology and Eschatology of the* Iḥyā'. Leiden, 2001.

Hillenbrand, Carole. '1092: A Murderous Year'. In Alexander Fodor (ed.), *Proceedings of the 14th Congress of the Union Européenne de Arabisants et Islamisants: The Arabist, Budapest Studies in Arabic*, 15–16 (1995), pp. 281–296.

Hindī, ʿAlā al-Dīn al-Muttaqī, al-. *Kanz al-ʿummāl*. Aleppo, 1389-1404/1969-1984.

Hodgson, Marshall G. S. *The Order of Assassins*. The Hague, 1955.

Hourani, G., 'The Chronology of Ghazālī's Writings'. *Journal of the American Oriental Society*, LXXIX (1959), pp. 225–231.

Ibn ʿAbd al-Barr, Yūsuf. *al-Istīʿāb fī maʿrifat al-aṣḥāb*. With *al-Iṣāba* of ʿAsqalānī. Cairo, 1359/1940.

Ibn Ghaylān and Ibn Sīnā. *Ḥudūth al-ʿālam and al-Ḥukūmāt*. Ed. M. Mohaghegh. Tehran, 1998.

Ibn al-Jawzī, ʿAbd al-Raḥmān. *Talbīs Iblīs*. Eds. Muḥammad b. al-Ḥasan ibn Ismāʿīl and Masʿad ʿAbd al-Ḥamīd al-Saʿdanī. Beirut, 1418/1998.

Ibn Sīnā. *al-Risāla al-aḍḥawiyya fī 'l-maʿād*. Ed. S. Dunyā. Cairo, 1328/1949.

———*al-Ishārāt wa 'l-tanbīhāt*. Ed. S. Dunyā. Beirut, 1413/1993.

Ibn Taymiyya, Aḥmad. *K. al-Nubuwwāt*. Riyadh, 1346/1927.

Iṣfahānī, Abū Nuʿaym, al-. *Ḥilyat al-awliyā' wa-ṭabaqāt al-aṣfiyā'*. Cairo, 1351-7/1932-8.

Jabre, F. *La Notion de la certitude selon Ghazālī*. Paris, 1958.

Jarrāḥī, Ismāʿīl ibn Muḥammad, al-. *Kashf al-khafā' wa muzīl al-ilbās*. Ed. Aḥmad al-Qallāsh. Aleppo, 1394/1974.

Kurdī, M. A., al-. *K. Khulāṣat al-taṣnīf fī 'l-taṣawwuf*. See Ghazālī, al-, *K. Khulāṣat al-taṣnīf fī 'l-taṣawwuf*.

Landolt, H. 'Ghazālī and "Religionswissenschaft"'. *Asiatische Studien/Études Asiatiques*, XLV.1 (1991), pp. 19–72.

Lazarus-Yafeh, Hava. *Studies in al-Ghazzali*. Jerusalem, 1975.

Madelung, Wilferd and Mayer, Toby. *Struggling with the Philosopher—A Refutation of Avicenna's Metaphysics: A New Arabic Edition and English Translation of Muḥammad ibn ʿAbd al-Karīm ibn Aḥmad al-Shahrastānī's* Kitāb al-Muṣāraʿa. London, 2001.

Massignon, Louis. *Essay on the Origins of the Technical Language of Islamic Mysticism*. Tr. from French by B. Clark. Notre Dame, 1997.

———*Hallāj: Mystic and Martyr*. Tr. from French and ed. by Herbert Mason. Princeton, 1982.

Maydānī, Aḥmad ibn Muḥammad, al-. *Majmaʿ al-amthāl*. Ed. Muḥammad ʿAbd al-Ḥamīd. Cairo, 1374/1955.

McCarthy, R. J. *Freedom and Fulfillment: An Annotated Translation of al-Ghazālī's* Al-Munqidh min al-Ḍalāl *and other Relevant Works of Al-Ghazālī*. Boston, 1980.

Michot, J. R., 'La Pandémie Avicennienne au VIe/XIIe Siècle'. *Arabica*, XL (1993), pp. 287–344.

Otto, R. *The Idea of the Holy*. Oxford, 1958.

Pasnau, R., 'Henry of Ghent and the Twilight of Divine Illumination'. *Review of Metaphysics*, 49 (1995), pp. 49–75.

Pertsch, Wilhelm. *Die Arabischen Handschriften der herzoglichen Bibliothek zu Gotha*. Gotha, 1878–1892. 5 vols.

Pourjavady, N. 'Minor Persian Works', *s.v.* *Ġazālī*, in Ehsan Yarshater (ed.), *Encyclopædia Iranica* (New York, 2001), vol. X, pp. 369–372.

Qushayrī, Abū 'l-Qāsim, al-. *al-Risāla fī ʿilm al-taṣawwuf*. Eds. A. Maḥmūd and M. al-Sharīf. Cairo, 1385/1966.

Rahman, Fazlur. *Prophecy in Islam: Philosophy and Orthodoxy*. Chicago and London, 1958.

Sabbagh, T. *Lettre au Disciple*. Ar. ed. and French trans. of *Ayyuhā 'l-Walad*. Beirut, 1959.

Scherer, G. H. *O Youth*. Beirut, 1933.

Sharif, M. M. (ed.). *A History of Muslim Philosophy*. Wiesbaden, 1963. 2 vols.

Sherif, M. A. *Ghazali's Theory of Virtue*. Albany, 1975.

Smith, Margaret. *Al-Ghazālī the Mystic*. London, 1994.

Sviri, Sara. 'Ḥakīm Tirmidhī and the *Malāmatī* Movement in Early Sufism'. In L. Lewisohn (ed.), *Classical Persian Sufism: from its Origins to Rumi*. London, 1993. pp. 583–613.

Walker, Paul E. *Early Philosophical Shiism: The Ismaili Neoplatonism of Abū Yaʿqūb al-Sijistānī*. Cambridge, 1993.

———*Ḥamīd al-Dīn al-Kirmānī: Ismaili Thought in the Age of al-Ḥākim*. London, 1999.

Watt, W. M., 'The Authenticity of the Works Attributed to al-Ghazālī'. *Journal of the Royal Asiatic Society* (1952), pp. 24–45.

———'A Forgery in al-Ghazālī's *Mishkāt*?' *Journal of the Royal Asiatic Society* (1949), pp. 5–22.

Winter, T. J. *Al-Ghazālī on Disciplining the Soul and on Breaking the Two Desires*. Cambridge, 1995. [Trans. of Books XXII and XXIII of the *Revival*.]

Zabīdī, al-Sayyid Muḥammad Murtaḍā, al-. *K. Itḥāf al-sādāt al-muttaqīn bi-sharḥ asrār* Iḥyā' ʿulūm al-dīn. Egypt, 1311/1893. 10 vols.

Index

ʿAbd Allāh ibn ʿUmar, 20
Abū Bakr al-Ṣiddīq, xxix, 18
ʿadhāb al-qabr ('the Punishment of the Grave'), xxv, 16
ʿAlī ibn Abī Ṭālib, xvii, xxx, xxxv, 12
al-amr bi 'l-maʿrūf wa nahy ʿan al-munkar('commanding the good and forbidding the evil'), xxxiv, 48
ʿaqabāt al-nafs ('obstructions of the ego'), xxvii*n*
ʿaqliyāt ('truths of reason'), xii–xiv
Ashʿarism, Ashʿarites, vii, xvi, xxx, xxxi, xxxviii
astronomy, 14
Avicenna, Avicennism, vii, viii, xvi–xviii, xviii*n*, xxii, xxvi, xxxvii, 6*n*

Baghdad, xi, xvi, xviii, xxi, xxxviii
al-Balkhī, Ibn Ghaylān, xxxvii
al-Balkhī, Shaqīq, xxxii, 28, 34
al-Baṣrī, al-Ḥasan, xxxi, 10, 12, 18
al-Basṭāmī, Abū Yazīd, ix
bidʿa ('innovation'), xxxiii, 26
Bouyges, Maurice, xxxv, xxxvii

'Cartesian circle', xv
chiasmus, xxviii, xxix
commanding the good and forbidding the evil, *see al-amr bi 'l-maʿrūf*

Davidson, H. A., 6*n*
Day of Resurrection, xxv, 6, 10, 16, 20, 42, 48, 60
Daylam, viii
Descartes, René, xiv, xv, xxxviii
dhawq ('direct experience', 'tasting'), xv, xvii*n*, xx, xxi*n*, xxii, xxiii, xxvii, xxxii, 24
dhikr Allāh, xix, xxvii*n*, 44
dogmas, *see taqlīdiyāt*

eklampsis (divine 'effulgence'), xv*n*
Ethé, H., xxxvi
eudæmonia ('well-being', 'happiness'), xxvi, 6

Faḍā'iḥ al-Bāṭiniyya, xvi, xxxvii
Fakhr al-Mulk, xxii
fanā' ('self-extinction', 'passing away'), x

al-Fārābī, Abū Naṣr, 6
al-Fārisī, ʿAbd al-Ghāfir, xvi
al-Farmadhī, Abū ʿAlī, xvi
Franciscans, xv*n*

Gospels, xxviii, xxxiv, 16, 34, 62
grammar, xxx, 14
guide, *see murshid*

al-Ḥaddādī, Abū Ḥafs ʿAmr, ix
Ḥadīth ('prophetic Tradition'), ix, xii
al-Ḥallāj, Manṣūr, ix, x
al-Hamadhānī, ʿAyn al-Quḍāt, ix
al-Ḥasan ibn al-Ṣabbāḥ, viii
Ḥātim al-Aṣamm, xxxii, 28
Ḥaydar Āmulī, Sayyid, xxxviii
ḥikma ('wisdom'), vii–ix
ḥilm ('mildness'), xxxiii, 36, 38
Ḥirā', xxi
Holy Law, *see* Sharīʿa
Hourani, George, xxiii, xxxviii
al-Hujwīrī, ʿAlī, xxxvii

Ibn Sīnā, *see* Avicenna, Avicennism
ʿĪd al-Aḍḥā, 22
Iḥyā' ʿulūm al-dīn ('The Revival of the Religious Sciences'), vii, xix, xx, xxii, 2, 26, 54, 58
ikhlāṣ ('sincerity'), xxxiii, 40
ʿilm aḥwāl al-qalb ('science of the states of the heart'), xx, xxvii, 58
Imām al-Ḥaramayn, *see* al-Juwaynī
inception, viii
Incoherence of the Philosophers, the, *see Tahāfut al-falāsifa*
initiatic chain, *see silsila*
innovation, *see bidʿa*
instauration, viii
ʿIrāqī, Fakhr al-Dīn, xxxviii
Ismāʿīlism, vii, viii, xvi, xviii, xxxviii
Israel, Tribe of, 12
iṣṭilāḥāt ('technical terminology'), xxii, xxvii, xxxiii

Jesus Christ, 16, 46, 48
al-Junayd, Junaydī, vii, x, xxvi, xxx, xxxvii, 6
al-Juwaynī, Abū 'l-Maʿālī ʿAbd al-Malik, xvi

al-Kalābādhī, Abū Bakr, xxxvii
Kalām (Muslim scholastic theology), ix, xviii, xxiv, xxxiv, 14, 56
Kāshānī, Mullā Muḥsin Fayḍ, xx
al-Khaḍir, 40
al-Khalīl, Ghulām, x
khalwa ('retreat'), xix, xxi
khānqāh, xxii
al-Kirmānī, Ḥamīd al-Dīn, viii

Luqmān, 22

maḥsūsāt ('sense data'), xii, xv
majestas, xxxv
al-Makkī, Abū Ṭālib, xxxvii
Malāmatī, ix

al-Maqdisī, Naṣr, xix
Massignon, Louis, ix*n*, xxxvii
Māzandarān, viii
metrics, 14
mildness, *see* *ḥilm*
Mishkāt al-anwār, xvii*n*, xxii*n*, xxvi
al-Miṣrī, Dhū 'l-Nūn, xxvii, 42
Mīzān al-ʿamal, xvi, xvii*n*
moral introspection, *see* *murāqabat al-qalb*
muḥāsabat al-nafs ('self-evaluation'), 62
mujaddid ('renewer'), vii
Munkar and Nakīr, 16, 48
al-Munqidh min al-ḍalāl, xii, xii*n*, xvii, xviii, xviii*n*, xx, xxi*n*, xxii, xxvii*n*, xxxvii, xxxviii
murāqabat al-qalb ('moral introspection'), xxxiv, 56
murshid ('spiritual guide'), xxiii, xxvii, xxix, xxxiii, 34
al-Murtaḍā, al-Sayyid, xxxv
al-Mustaẓhir bi-'Llāh, xvi
Muʿtazilism, xxx

Nakīr and Munkar, *see* Munkar and Nakīr
al-Nassāj, Yūsuf, xi
necessitarianism, xxxi, xxxiii, 10, 12
Nīshāpūr, xvi, xxii
Niẓām al-Mulk, *see* al-Ṭūsī
Niẓāmiyya colleges, xi, xvi, xviii, xxii
al-Nūrī, Abū 'l-Ḥusayn, ix

omnipotence, xiv, xxxi, 40, 60
orgê theoû ('divine anger'), xxxv
Otto, Rudolf, xxxv

Palamas, St. Gregory, xv*n*
Pertsch, Wilhelm, xxxvi
philosophy, philosophers, viii, xiv–xviii, xviii*n*, xxxvii, xxxviii, 6
Pillars of Islam, xxxi, 10, 10*n*
preacher, xxiv, xxv, xxxiv, 48, 50
prophetic Tradition, *see* *Ḥadīth*
Psalms, 34
Punishment of the Grave, *see* *ʿadhāb al-qabr*

al-Qaṣṣār, Ḥamdūn, ix
al-Qawārīrī, *see* al-Junayd
al-Quddūs, Ṣāliḥ ibn ʿAbd, xiii*n*
Qūhistān, viii
quietism, xxvii, xxxiii
al-Qushayrī, Abū 'l-Qāsim, xvi

al-Radhkānī, Aḥmad, xi
Ramaḍān, 10
reliance on God, *see* *tawakkul*
renewer, *see* *mujaddid*
Resurrection, *see* Day of Resurrection
Revival of the Religious Sciences, *see* *Iḥyā' ʿulūm al-dīn*
rhetoric, xxx, 14
riyā' ('eyeservice'), xxxiii, 40, 42

Sabbāgh, Toufic, xxiii*n*, xxvi, xxvii

Saʿd ibn Muʿādh, 18
sajʿ ('rhyming prose'), xxviii
Salafī, ix
al-Sarrāj, Abū Naṣr, xxxvii
Satan, 32, 38, 52
scepticism, xii, xiii, xiii*n*, xiv, xv
Scherer, G.H., xxiii*n*, xxvi, xxxv*n*
science of the states of the heart, *see* *ʿilm aḥwāl al-qalb*
Seljuq, vii–ix, xi, xiii, xvi, xix, xx, xxii
sense data, *see* *maḥsūsāt*
Shāfiʿism, Shāfiʿite, vii, xi
al-Shahrastānī, Muḥammad ibn ʿAbd al-Karīm, xxxvii
Sharīʿa, xxvi, xxx, xxxii, 14, 22, 24, 52
shaṭḥ ('theopathic utterance'), x, xxvi, 6, 24
al-Shiblī, Abū Bakr, xxxii, 26
Shīʿism, vii, viii, xx
al-Ṣiddīq, *see* Abū Bakr
al-Sijistānī, Abū Yaʿqūb, viii
silsila ('initiatic chain'), xxxiii, 36
al-Simnānī, ʿAlā' al-Dawla, xxxviii
sincerity, *see* *ikhlāṣ*
skepsis, *see* scepticism
sober (versus 'intoxicated') mysticism, vii, x, xxvi
sola gratia, xxx
Sufism, vii–xi, xv, xix–xxi, xxvi, xxvii, xxxiii, xxxiv, 38, 58*n*
Sufyān al-Thawrī, 20
al-Sulamī, Abū ʿAbd al-Raḥmān, xxxvii
Sumnūn ibn Ḥamza, ix

Tahāfut al-falāsifa, xvi, xxxvii
taʿlīm ('authoritative instruction'), xvii*n*, xviii
taqlīdiyāt ('dogmas'), xii
ṭarīqa, pl. *ṭuruq* ('Sufi order'), xx
tashrīq, ayām al-, 22
tawakkul ('reliance on God'), xxxiii, 36, 38
technical terminology, *see* *iṣṭilāḥāt*
al-Thawrī, *see* Sufyān al-Thawrī
theopathic utterance, *see* *shaṭḥ*
theôsis, x
Torah, 34
truths of reason, *see* *ʿaqliyāt*
Ṭūs, xi, xxii
al-Ṭūsī, Abū ʿAlī Ḥasan, xi, xvi, xxii

ʿubūdiyya ('servanthood'), xxxiii, 38, 54
ʿulamā' (the Muslim scholarly class), xxv

waḥdat al-shuhūd, xxvi
Wahhābī, ix
wisdom, *see* *ḥikma*